W9-APM-834

TAKING
CHARGE
OF
CHANGE

Shirley M. Hord
William L. Rutherford
Leslie Huling-Austin
Gene E. Hall

Association for Supervision and Curriculum Development
125 N. West Street, Alexandria, Virginia 22314-2798
703-549-9110

Copyright 1987 by the Southwest Educational Development Laboratory.

All rights reserved. No part of this publication may be reproduced or transmitted in any form or by any means, electronic or mechanical, including photocopy, recording, or any information storage and retrieval system, without permission in writing from SEDL (211 East 7th Street, Austin, TX 78710).

ASCD Stock Number: 611-87022
ISBN: 0-87120-144-5
Library of Congress Catalog Card Number: 87-070644
$8.00

ASCD publications present a variety of viewpoints. The views expressed or implied in this publication are not necessarily official positions of the Association.

Taking Charge of Change

Foreword

ONE HAS ONLY TO SEARCH OBSCURE STORAGE CLOSETS OR BOOKROOMS in schools or talk with those who have been involved with education and its improvement over a period of time to understand the frustration involved in changing the status quo. Innovations involved with instructional strategies and curriculums have usually failed. Remember the promises held by many for open classrooms, team teaching, educational television, new math, and inquiry-oriented science?

But did these innovations fail because the concepts and processes proposed were faulty? Or because they were never properly implemented? We will never know. Evaluations of innovations have usually focused on the assessment of their effectiveness. This type of assessment, without an examination of how the innovation was implemented, leads to distorted results.

One of the most common and serious mistakes made by both the administrators and leaders of a change process is to presume that once an innovation has been introduced and initial training has been completed the intended users will put the innovation into practice. A second serious mistake is to assume that all users of the implementation will react in similar ways.

Taking Charge of Change

This book provides new insights and understandings about school change. Its powerful message brings a new understanding about the roles and personal needs of the people involved in a change process. It hits at the heart of the problem by providing strategies for the total management of an innovation destined for success.

The first strategy presented provides the means to both introduce the change or innovation and monitor the anticipated variety and diversity of implementation. The Innovation Configuration leads to the development of component checklists that are useful in determining an accurate picture of the range of operational patterns that could be found in classrooms.

The second strategy focuses on the target of the change process, the teacher. A diagnostic approach identifies seven stages of concern experienced by teachers involved in a change process. Suggestions are given to deliver interventions that will respond to each stage of concern.

The concept of the levels of use of the innovation provides the third strategy, which identifies the degree to which teachers are using the new practices. This tool is useful for assisting teachers to move to higher levels of use as well as for evaluating the progress of the implementation effort.

One of the major contentions of this book is that guesswork and intuition need not be the tools used by individuals responsible for the process of change. The specific role played by those individuals and the orchestration of their efforts is presented with six areas of actions that support a change process.

Taking Charge of Change provides diagnostic techniques for assessing the individuals involved in a change in order to understand both them and their needs. Those techniques then provide the agents of the change process with information about how to use resources and provide support services. This book carries a powerful message for all success-oriented agents of change.

Marcia Kalb Knoll
ASCD President, 1987-88

1.
You Are In This Book

In Springdale School District, student achievement scores had declined for five years. Alarmed, the school board directed Julia Jenkins, the assistant superintendent for instruction, to develop a plan and recommend ways of turning the scores around.Jenkins, too, had been concerned and had been looking into some ways to address the problem. After exploring a number of alternatives, she prepared to introduce an effective teaching program used by a number of other districts in the area. In this program, teachers consider particular instructional decisions when planning and delivering instruction. Furthermore, teaching is structured in a step-by-step approach that has effectively increased student learning. Jenkins found that participating administrators and teachers in the other districts were enthusiastic about the program. They believed they were starting to see improvements in student learning as a result of its use.

Jenkins and two elementary and two secondary instructional coordinators attended a week-long training session to learn firsthand how teachers could be trained in the skills of the effective teaching program. When they returned to Springdale they were enthusiastic about introducing it in their district. Assistant Superintendent Jenkins recommended to the school board that the district make a three-year commitment to implementing the new program. "Three years!" The school board president could not understand the need for devoting three years to *bringing the program to teachers. "Didn't we do science in nine months last year?" After an intense four-hour discussion, the board reluctantly appropriated 60 percent of the requested funds to support the program, instructing Jenkins to proceed with the program with teachers at all grade levels. It was to be Jenkins's program, and the board wanted regular reports of its results.*

With the board's directive, Jenkins became responsible for a school improvement effort.

IN THIS SCENARIO, WE SEE AND FEEL JULIA JENKINS'S QUANDARY. SOME of us know it from our own experiences; others can foresee it in their own future. In this hypothetical case study we see a program that promises to improve the instructional practices of teachers, and thus increase learning outcomes for students, but one that is allotted barely sufficient time and support for integration in classrooms. The program is sure to seesaw between pressures for immediate results urged by the board and demands of time, energy, and actions needed for its successful implementation. "Why three years?" the board asks. Clearly Jenkins must "school" the board in understanding just what is required for effective school change and improvement. At the same time, she faces a pressing demand to mobilize resources and people—there is not a moment of the three years to waste.

Why This Book

You are in this book.

In your professional life you have been or will be involved in processes of institutional change—as a manager, as a person assisting the process, or as one expected to adopt an innovation. Primarily, this book is about and for people like Julia Jenkins who are responsible at the district level for improving schools, and for others at the school level who facilitate change in their schools; its concepts, however, touch the lives of each of us in the ever-changing world of education.

The focus is on change facilitators and on methods to make their job more effective. To these change facilitators we offer concepts, tools, and techniques.

This book, then, is written for each of you who wishes to become a more effective facilitator of change. It does not address directly the abstract concerns of scholars who observe and study school change, although we believe scholars may find the book's applications of research to be of interest, as will policymakers who must make decisions that thrust change on schools.

In this first chapter, we explain the term "change facilitator" and discuss who change facilitators are. We describe the components of the knowledge base that supports this book and relate how we had the opportunity to help develop this knowledge. In the last part of the chapter we share some early learnings and the conclusions on which our work rests; finally, we provide an overview of the remaining chapters.

Who Is a Change Facilitator?

A change facilitator can be anyone. You may be one yourself. Facilitators are found in central offices of school districts where they may be curriculum coordinators or consultants; subject specialists or directors; assistant, associate, or deputy superintendents; and perhaps (in small districts) even superintendents. Facilitators are also found at the school level among principals, vice principals, and assistant principals. Department chairs, mentor teachers, master teachers, grade-level chairs, or teachers on special assignment may be change facilitators. And teachers frequently relate to each other in less formal ways as facilitators.

It's not important where on the organizational chart the person falls; what is important is that facilitators support, help, assist, and nurture. Sometimes their task is to encourage, persuade, or push people to change, to adopt an innovation and use it in their daily schooling work. ("Innovation" is our generic term for any program, process, or practice—new or not—that is new to a person). We have chosen the name for these supporters thoughtfully; we believe the term "facilitator" embodies the spirit and behaviors of the tasks mentioned above. Some would use the label "change agent." We prefer "change facilitator," as we believe this person, in working directly with people who are expected to change, must engage this very human challenge in a personalized, caring way. For brevity, we frequently refer to the change facilitator as the "CF."

Interestingly, we observe school improvement efforts in which facilitators are not clearly identified. Central office staff may think a principal is the CF, while the principal may believe this role resides in the central office. A basic tenet of successful change management is that someone must be in charge, the locus of control for the change process must be clearly identified, and the facilitator must be skilled and prepared to act.

If your dilemma is that you do not have the requisite skills or know what to do, then this book is for you. Our goal is to help you acquire some basic understandings and skills to facilitate change in your school setting.

How We Got Started

For more than a decade, we worked in an uncommon alliance, centered on federally funded research conducted at the Research and

Development Center for Teacher Education (R&DCTE), at the University of Texas at Austin. Along with other other colleagues, we engaged in a collaborative enterprise to learn how schools might go about the process of changing. We did not focus on what schools should do; there has long been a ready supply of research-based advice on that matter. What we were about was an unflinching pursuit to learn about the school improvement *process*; what it is, whom it involves, what are its effects, and how it might be managed. Our findings integrate research studies on teachers and administrators, are seasoned by our experiences in classrooms and schools, and are refined with craft knowledge and clinical judgment.

In addition, we have been fortunate to study and plan for school improvement with international colleagues. We have worked with schools, school administrators, and researchers in Australia, Belgium, Canada, England, France, Germany, Italy, Japan, The Netherlands, Norway, Sweden, and Switzerland, all in settings where attention and concern is being focused on improving teachers' and administrators' practice. We have looked through different lenses at school improvement and have gained insights from different cultures and perspectives. These experiences have sharpened our images of our own schools. What we share, then, is both experience-based and research-based, although we will not use this book as a research forum. We have sprinkled modest research citations throughout the book, but we determinedly kept them to a minimum. For those who seek to know more and at greater depth, the appendix provides relevant references.

Why was this team given an opportunity to study change in schools? The headwaters lie in the late '50s, when a critical school reform movement was launched with Sputnik, stimulating a major examination and assessment of U.S. schools. As a result, a great deal of time, energy, and fiscal resources were given to the development of new curriculums, primarily in mathematics and science. Accompanying this development effort was an innocent but unfortunate assumption that if a curriculum program was sufficiently appealing and attractively packaged, it could be delivered to teachers and, without further ado, the program would appear in their day-to-day classroom work (Hord 1987).

Some of you may remember the introduction of "new math" into schools in the early '60s. As classroom teachers at that time, we recall the math books being sent to our rooms, a quickie orientation to the textbooks supplied, and a "God bless you" bestowed upon us. The teacher's guide was permanently affixed to our arm. Nightly study for preparing the next day's lesson became the norm. The frustration of trying to use this radical new approach to mathematics—to enable students to understand mathematical operations rather than simply doing rote computing—caused many teachers to give up and return to their old, familiar texts.

By the time new, inquiry-oriented science curriculums were being sent to schools, an understanding dawned that teachers needed more than the "stuff" of the program. As a result, the National Science Foundation began to experiment with providing summer institutes for inservice training in using the materials and equipment.

Providing both the materials for new programs and training in their use was expected to make program implementation a certainty. One year after a new program was introduced, an evaluator typically appeared to find out how well students were learning as a function of the new curriculums. Great surprise and consternation followed the evaluation results, which usually reported no significant improvement in scores. The typical conclusion drawn from such discouraging data was that the program was not a good one. Thereafter, the program was rejected and a new one brought on board. Thus, an annual cycle developed: introduce a new curriculum, allow it one year, evaluate its results, and then discard it.

The introduction/evaluation/rejection cycle became so commonplace that after a few years teachers accepted this peculiar state of affairs. Upon hearing that yet another new program was on its way, they were wont to say, "Hang loose, this too will fade away." And many are still saying it.

Frustration mounted in the nation's schools until one day a bright idea dawned: "Hey, wait a minute, maybe the program isn't to blame; maybe there's a problem with the process being used to change schools." Thereupon, a decision was made to investigate this national dilemma. The federal government, through the National Institute of Education, funded studies to look into educational change and improvement processes in an effort to understand how change could become a successful enterprise.

What We Have Learned about Change

Our R&DCTE team was awarded the opportunity to study how schools might go about improving successfully. In doing so, we verified a number of assumptions about change that were the basis of a model upon which our research was founded: the Concerns-Based Adoption Model (CBAM). Let us share these conclusions:

1. *Change is a process, not an event*. One of the most persistent tendencies of those who do not appreciate the complexities of change is to equate change with handing over a new program, which is an event. This, in fact, was the false tenet on which school improvement was

based in the past. We now know that change is a process occurring over time, usually a period of several years. Recognition of this is an essential prerequisite of successful implementation of change.

2. _Change is accomplished by individuals_. A common notion in considering change is to think about it in ambiguous, impersonal terms. But change affects people, and their role in the process is of utmost importance. Therefore, individuals must be the focus of attention in implementing a new program. Only when each (or almost each) individual in the school has absorbed the improved practice can we say that the school has changed.

3. _Change is a highly personal experience_. What we mean here is that individuals are different; people do not behave collectively. Each individual reacts differently to a change, and sufficient account of these differences must be taken. Some people will assimilate a new practice much more rapidly than others; some will engage in the process more readily than. Change will be most successful when its support is geared to the diagnosed needs of the individual users. If change is highly personal, then clearly different responses and interventions will be required for different individuals. Paying attention to each individual's progress can enhance the improvement process.

4. _Change involves developmental growth_. We have discovered from studies of change that the individuals involved appear to express or demonstrate growth in terms of their feelings and skills. These feelings and skills tend to shift with respect to the new program or practice as individuals pass through an ever-greater degree of experience. We will consider these feelings and skills in the pages that follow as we see that they can be diagnosed and prescribed for. The techniques for doing so are presented in this book, and they are valuable tools for school leaders and other change facilitators to use in guiding and managing change.

5. _Change is best understood in operational_ terms. Teachers, and others, will naturally relate to change or improvement in terms of what it will mean to them or how it will affect their current classroom practice. What changes in their own or their students' values, beliefs, and behavior will it require? How much preparation time will it demand? By addressing these and other questions in concrete, practical terms, facilitators can communicate more relevantly and reduce resistance to improvement efforts.

6. _The focus of facilitation should be on individuals, innovations, and the context_. We tend to see school improvement in terms of a new curriculum, a new program or package—something concrete that we can hold onto. But in doing so, we forget that books and materials and equipment alone do not make change; only people can make change by altering their behavior. The real meaning of any change lies in its human, not its

material, component. Furthermore, effective change facilitators work with people in an adaptive and systemic way, designing interventions for clients' needs, realizing that those needs exist in particular contexts and settings. Functioning in a systemic way recognizes that the school as a whole will be affected by whatever is done with respect to even its smallest part. Interventions in one arena may well produce unexpected results in another. Therefore, notions about the speed with which successful school improvement can be accomplished, the specific actions needed to achieve it, and even the shape that implemented change will ultimately take may have to be altered along the way.

In summary, because the CBAM model is client-centered, it can identify the special needs of individual users and enable the change facilitator to provide vital assistance through appropriate actions. This approach helps to maximize the prospects for successful school improvement projects while minimizing the innovation-related frustrations of individuals.

A Few More Observations about School Change

School change can have vastly different meanings to educators in individual schools, districts, and countries. Indeed, we have observed these differences across the constituent groups within a school community and certainly within a single country. One of our cross-national observations has been the different meanings that the term "school improvement" connotes. In Japan, for instance, school improvement seems to be viewed as permeating all activities, focusing on steadily becoming better, in all ways and in all things. School improvement is perceived as "a way of life." The Swedish view is concerned with altering the overall ethos and aims of the schools. In North America, however, school improvement appears to be associated with specific, frequently single-focused or single-subject curriculum initiatives introduced by local school districts, with increasing input from the state level. Because U.S. school improvement efforts have traditionally translated into the adoption of such curriculum innovations, the CBAM work has addressed this topic, and this book contains useful insights into the process.

A second observation that seems worthy of sharing involves the issue of bottom-up versus top-down change strategies. The word "versus" reflects this issue and the typical bias that persons engaged in the debate about these two different approaches express. We do not engage in the debate except to observe that we have seen both aproaches work successfully. Obviously a change or improvement endeavor that originates with a single teacher or small group of teachers, who believe in the change and persuade the entire faculty of the worthiness of the change, has the advantage of a committed core of teachers.

When change begins at a higher level—at the principal's desk or in the district's central office—there is a different kind of advantage: the possibility for more change to occur more rapidly if appropriate kinds of interventions are provided. We have seen both approaches result in effective change and in improved practices in the classroom, school, and school district. The important factor in all cases, whether at the single teacher level or at the level of all teachers across a district is the support and assistance provided to make the change. If properly facilitated, both strategies can work.

An Overview of the Book

We have structured this book and developed its chapters in a way that we hope is practical and provides the reader a clear sense of the CBAM and its applications. We have chosen to thread the chapters together by means of the story of Springdale School District, a district that could be urban, suburban, or rural, and (with slight modifications) be of any size. By using the story, we hope to make the messages of each chapter more concrete and more relevant to the reader. Springdale does not represent a specific school district, although it could; rather, it is a composite of many schools and districts we have known. We considered using a different school story for each chapter, but because some explanation of each school's context would be necessary, we decided to save space by retaining the same school district throughout. We should note that while some schools, such as Springdale, use the whole CBAM model, most schools select those dimensions of the model they deem most useful to their particular situation.

So that you might know in advance the book's sequence or in case you wish to jump and sample around, we offer here a brief description of each of the chapters.

Chapter Two. The Various Forms of an Innovation. Innovation Configurations (IC), one component of the CBAM, is a tool that can be used for introducing change and monitoring its implementation. This tool focuses on identifying and describing the various forms of an innovation (or an "improvement" identified for implementation) that different teachers adopt. Innovations are almost always altered by individual teachers to fit the conditions and needs of their students and classrooms. By using IC, innovation component checklists can be developed to identify and describe the various operational patterns of innovations that could be found in classrooms. Sample checklists are used to show how to apply this concept in introducing, communicating, and monitoring implementation of a new school improvement practice.

Chapter Three. From the Teacher's Perspective. A primary diagnostic concept that forms a basic tool of the CBAM is one that focuses on the "concerns" that teachers experience during change efforts. These concerns range from early self-concerns to task and ultimately affect concerns about change. In chapter three, the seven Stages of Concern are introduced and explained. Illustrations of teachers' concerns are also included. Readers are guided in how to identify Stages of Concern and shown how to use this diagnostic tool in everyday practice.

Chapter Four. Use of an Innovation in Classrooms. A third diagnostic tool comes from the concept of Levels of Use. These Levels of Use portray the way teachers and others work with innovations or new school improvement practices. Levels of Use can identify those teachers who are actually employing the new practices efficiently, those who are still experimenting with them, and those who have not yet started. The eight levels are described and illustrated to give readers a basic understanding of the concept and how to assess Levels of Use as part of daily interactions with teachers.

Chapter Five. The Role of Effective Change Facilitators. In this chapter the emphasis is on "game planning" for an overall implementation effort, based on an understanding of Stages of Concern, Levels of Use, and Innovation Configurations. We describe how six functional areas of interventions are provided by a team of change facilitators. Principals are not the only players; others (such as teachers, internal resource persons, and external support people) also play major roles. How these individuals work together to provide the necessary facilitation for those involved in changing is the primary thrust of this chapter. It also demonstrates uses of the ideas and techniques presented in previous chapters.

Finally, we present the CBAM's implications for school management and policy development in a brief conclusion to this book that contains important messages for all who are interested in educational innovation and the improvement of schools.

For readers who appreciate graphic overviews of such models and their parts, see Figure 1.1, which organizes the CBAM phenomena that will be described in chapters two through five.

In Figure 1.1, note the position of the change facilitator (CF) in the framework and this person's central importance. The CF is a major factor in the CBAM model and is a person or persons who deliver actions based on the needs of the individuals (denoted by "i" in the drawing) or groups of individuals involved in change and improvement. Facilitators have a resource system available to help individuals change. The re-

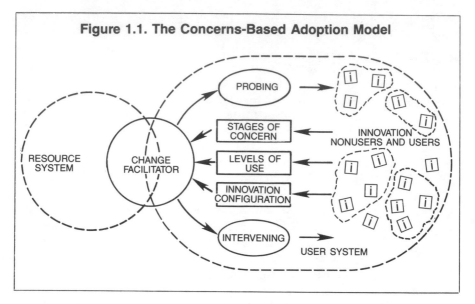

Figure 1.1. The Concerns-Based Adoption Model

sources may be rich or quite thin. Which resources and how and when to use them is grounded in a "concerns-based diagnosis."

For the diagnosis, the CF uses various techniques for probing the people involved in order to understand them and their needs; such diagnosis can be accomplished through use of Stages of Concern, Levels of Use, and Innovation Configurations. The hypothesis underlying the CBAM model suggests that with diagnostic information the CF can make decisions about how to use resources and provide interventions to individuals to facilitate the school improvement process. This book will show you how to be a change facilitator and how to make the model work for you.

2.
The Various Forms of an Innovation

In Springdale, Assistant Superintendent Jenkins believed it important for all administrators to be knowledgeable about the new effective teaching program. For this reason administrators would receive advance training before teachers would be expected to use the program. She arranged to have program trainers come to the district and conduct a training session for the entire central office instructional staff and all principals in the district. Teachers received training during the summer, and began using the program in the fall.

By October, it became clear to Jenkins that many teachers were uncertain about how the program was to be used. Teachers in one elementary school complained that the new approach was too time consuming, that restructuring all their lesson plans into the new format was creating too much paperwork, and that the approach was so structured that it was stifling their creativity. The secondary coordinators reported that many high school teachers had not changed their teaching practice because it was their understanding that they could choose whether to use or not to use the program. Both the elementary and secondary coordinators reported that teachers were upset when they received a classroom visit because they thought only "weak" teachers were being targeted for visits and were expected to use the program.

In fact, several teachers had mentioned that they thought the district was penalizing the group for the shortcomings of a few by requiring everyone to attend the training session. Finally, Jenkins was especially distressed to hear that one principal had told his faculty not to worry about the program, that the teaching approach recommended was mostly common sense, and that good teachers were already doing most of it anyway.

SPRINGDALE'S SITUATION ILLUSTRATES THE COMMON DIFFICULTY IN communicating to all teachers clear and consistent information about the specific elements of a new program and expectations for its use. Moreover, even when clear information is shared with teachers, you, the facilitator, will often find extensive variations in how teachers implement a new program in their individual classrooms. For example, a new reading program may consist of a textbook, a set of supplementary materials, a record-keeping system, and a set of assessment tests. One teacher may use all pieces of the program in exactly the ways the inservice trainer suggested they be used. A second teacher may use the textbook but not the supplementary materials, use some of the assessment tests, and modify the record-keeping system. A third teacher may use only the textbook.

It is important for a number of reasons for you as a facilitator to be able to identify the specific ways in which teachers put a program into operation. (You can help yourself in this task, and greatly improve teachers' understanding of their tasks, by always communicating in specific operational terms what the program is to look like in classroom practice.) Once implementation is under way, you must be able to identify exactly what specific teachers are doing with the program in order to determine how best to assist them. For example, in the reading program example described above, the teacher who is using only the textbook needs a completely different type of assistance than the teacher who is using all parts of the program. You will also need detailed information about how the program is being implemented to be able to report with confidence to parents, school board members, and others. Finally, before you can consider student outcome data in an attempt to answer the question of how well a certain program works, you must be certain to what degree the program actually has been implemented. It is impossible to determine whether a program has merit if, in fact, it has been poorly or only partially implemented.

The Concept of Innovation Configurations

The concept of Innovation Configurations (Hall and Loucks 1981) emerged from our research on the change process. In our studies, we often attempted to answer the question, "How are teachers using X Program?" It soon became obvious that we needed to address a prior question: "What exactly is X program?"

Answering this question is not always as straightforward as it might seem. Often educational programs are defined in terms of their attributes, ultimate goals, or implementation requirements. One might describe a new program in general terms such as "It's easy to use," or "It's been shown to increase student achievement," or "It's fun and students enjoy it." Such statements may be helpful in some ways, but they do not help the teacher to know what to do with the program.

Describing a program in terms of its ultimate goals also offers little help with the task of implementation. For example, an art program might be intended to develop stronger relationships between teachers and the local art museum, thus encouraging students to visit the museum and bring their parents. While teachers need to be aware of the purpose of what they are doing, goals alone cannot tell them how to implement the program in the classroom. Implementation requirements are another common, but inadequate, way of describing programs. A computer program might require that teachers attend four days of training and that each classroom be equipped with ten student terminals. Again, these requirements are important, but do little to specify how the program is to be operated.

While attributes, goals, and implementation requirements are important, we believe it is critical to be able to talk about an educational program in clear, operational terms. To be truly helpful to teachers, you must be able to describe how a program will look in actual practice in the classroom. This concern guided our research and led to the development of the concept of Innovation Configurations.

Innovation Configurations (IC) represents the patterns of innovation use that result when different teachers put innovations into operation in their classrooms. In the course of our early work, we noted that individual teachers (and professors) used different parts of an innovation in different ways. When these parts were put together, a number of patterns emerged, each characterizing a different use of the innovation. We called these patterns Innovation Configurations. We developed a tool, the IC component checklist (Heck, Stiegelbauer, Hall, and Loucks 1981), for use in identifying the components, or parts, of an innovation and variations in the use of each part. This procedure has helped to answer the question "What is it?" Before we focus our attention on the checklist, however, it is important to explain some of the basic terms we use in talking about IC.

Terminology Related to IC

We use the term *component* to mean the major operational features or parts of any innovation. With instructional innovations, component descriptions are usually based on materials, teacher behaviors, and student activities. A simple example would be a continuous progress math program with three components:

Component 1: Use of instructional materials
Component 2: Grouping of students
Component 3: Testing and use of test results

A language arts program might consist of the following four components:

Component 1: Use of sequenced program objectives
Component 2: Use of program materials
Component 3: Use of prescribed writing process
Component 4: Student recording of writing progress

In some programs, those components that have been determined to be essential to innovation use are designated as *critical*. Other, *related* components are not considered essential to the innovation but are recommended by the developer or facilitator as "nice to have." Designation of a component as critical or related can be done by a developer, change facilitator, user, or evaluator, preferably through a consensus-reaching process involving all these persons. Also, the designations may change during the life cycle of the innovation. For example, in the case of the continuous progress math program, the facilitator may decide that during the first year of use, only component 1 (use of program materials) is critical. In other words, teachers must use the program materials, but they may choose to use or not to use components 2 and 3. As implementation progresses and teachers use component 1 successfully, however, the other two components will be given attention and perhaps be designated as critical.

Within each component, there are a number of possible *variations* that might be observed during implementation. Variations represent the different ways in which a teacher can put a component into operation in the classroom. Note the variations in each of the three components of the continuous progress math program:

Component 1: Use of instructional materials
 a. program materials only
 b. program materials plus basic text
 c. text only
 d. teacher-made materials only

Component 2: Grouping of students
  a. large, heterogeneous group
  b. large, homogeneous group
  c. small groups
  d. completely individualized

Component 3: Testing and use of test results
  a. testing once every six weeks but nothing done with test results
  b. testing weekly with test results fed back to students
  c. student self-testing upon completing each objective

As we have mentioned, configurations are the operational patterns of an innovation that result from implementation of different component variations. In the example above one teacher of the continuous progress math program might be teaching students as a large group using program materials plus the basic text (component 1, variation b), with testing done every six weeks but nothing done with test results (component 3, variation a). "Component 1, variation b; component 2, variation b; and component 3, variation a"; or "bba" represents this teacher's configuration. Other combinations of component variations represent other configurations. When configurations for a large number of teachers have been identified, it is possible to determine the most common ones and to identify the teachers who are using identical or similar configurations and those who are not. Again, this information is helpful in determining what types of assistance are most appropriate for specific teachers.

Another term that often comes up in relation to IC is that of *fidelity*. Often people assume that as developers of the IC concept, we must be proponents of strict fidelity, expecting teachers to use a program exactly as it was envisioned by an innovation developer. Actually, we do not take a stand on the fidelity issue; that is, we do not propose that one particular configuration of use of an innovation is what all teachers should be doing. We do, however, argue for the need for facilitators to be well informed about how teachers are using a program, whatever their use may be. It is up to the facilitators of each specific program to determine what "ideal" practice is and to determine how much variation from that ideal is acceptable.

More about IC Component Checklists

As mentioned earlier, the IC component checklist is a tool for identifying specific components or parts of an innovation and the variations that might be expected as the innovation is put into operation in classrooms or schools. An innovation-specific checklist should be developed for each program that is to be the focus of a school improvement effort. Once you have developed the checklist, you can use it to introduce the program and communicate how the components and variations might be phased in for classroom use. Once implementation is under way, you can use the checklist to monitor program progress by interviewing teachers about their use of the program and their typical classroom practice. During or immediately after each interview, you can complete an IC component checklist for each teacher by circling the number or letter of the variation that best describes that teacher's practice within each component.

The IC component checklist can be organized into various formats. The simplest format is to prepare the checklist in list or outline form, much as the continuous progress math program checklist was organized. You can use this checklist by simply placing a check mark by the appropriate variations. Another way of organizing the checklist is a left-to-right format, with the variations of each component organized across the page. Using this format, you can place the variation judged to be the ideal or most acceptable variation of each component in the far left column, with the other variations ranging in order of descending acceptability across the page so that the least desirable variation appears in the far right column. An example of an IC component checklist organized in the left-to-right format is shown in Figure 2.1. Note the use of the vertical dotted and solid lines to indicate ideal, acceptable, and unacceptable practice. Variations to the left of the dotted line are considered ideal. Variations located between the dotted and solid vertical lines are acceptable, though not ideal, and variations to the right of the solid line are unacceptable. This format provides a graphic picture of ideal or preferred practice, valuing some variations over others.

In constructing a checklist, you will find that there is no set number of components that an innovation should have and no set number of variations that a component should have. The number of components will be determined by the major parts of the innovation. Most innovations will have between three and eight major parts, although some complex innovations will contain more. Variations within components should represent meaningful differences in classroom practice and yet not be so numerous as to make it difficult to identify patterns of use. Generally, you will find three to five variations, although in some cases only two variations will exist (as in the case when something is or is not present). Occasionally you may identify more than five variations within a component.

You can identify components of an innovation and variations within components by reviewing written materials on the program and inter-

Figure 2.1. Tutoring Program Checklist

*1. Materials and Equipment

(1)	(2)	(3)
At least 5 different program materials are used with each child each session.	At least 3 different program materials are used with each child each session.	Fewer than 3 different program materials are used with each child each session.

*2. Diagnosis

(1)	(2)	(3)
Children are diagnosed individually using a combination of tests and teacher judgment.	Children are diagnosed individually using teacher judgment only.	Children are not diagnosed individually.

3. Record-Keeping

(1)	(2)
Individual record sheet is used to record diagnosis and prescription.	No individual record sheets are used.

*4. Use of Teaching Technique

(1)	(2)
Continually readjusts task according to child needs; uses rewards to reinforce success.	Does not continually readjust task according to child needs; does not use rewards.

5. Grouping

(1)	(2)
Children are taught in pairs.	Children are not taught in pairs.

*6. Scheduling

(1)	(2)	(3)
Children are taught for 30 minutes 3 times per week. Each session is equally divided between children.	Children are taught for 30 minutes 3 times per week, time for each child and each task varies slightly when necessary.	Children are not taught for 30 minutes per week 3 times per week, or time for each child and each task varies markedly or is not considered.

CODE: _____ Variations to the right are unacceptable; variations to the left are acceptable.

– – – – – Variations to the left are ideal, as prescribed by the developer.

* Denotes critical components.

From: Heck, Stiegelbauer, Hall, and Loucks 1981.

viewing the developer or some other authority on the program. From this information a preliminary checklist (often in the form of a list or outline) can be developed. This preliminary checklist can be useful in communicating what the program is and clarifying expectations for its use. If implementation is already under way when the preliminary checklist is developed, you can use it to observe and interview a small number of users to verify the initially identified components and variations and to identify others. Using the information gained through this initial data-gathering activity, you (often in collaboration with the developer/program authority) can then revise and expand the checklist to better reflect actual classroom practice. At this time, decisions are usually made about which variations are more desirable than others. The revised checklist then can be used to interview a larger number of users in different adopter sites, and further revisions can be made if necessary.

Constructing checklists is a complex task. One- and two-day workshops are available to train facilitators in developing skills in checklist construction. Our intent here is to introduce you to the concept of IC, the process of checklist development, and the application of the IC component checklist in facilitating the implementation of educational programs. For those of you who desire more in-depth information, we have included references at the end of the book.

IC and the Springdale Effective Teaching Program

When Springdale's Assistant Superintendent Jenkins began to realize that teachers felt uncertain about how the effective teaching program was to be used, she met with the instructional coordinators and later with school principals to discuss the matter. The discussions revealed that while everyone seemed to have a general understanding of the program, few people understood exactly what was expected of teachers in their use of the program in daily classroom practice. Jenkins realized that a large part of the confusion could have been avoided if she had prepared an IC component checklist at the outset. Certainly at this time it was important to develop an IC component checklist in order to communicate expectations about the program and how it was to be implemented.

Working with several of the instructional coordinators and the program trainer who had provided training for the district, Jenkins developed a preliminary checklist. In mid-November, she used the checklist to interview and observe a small sample of teachers. Using information gained from these interviews, she and the instructional coordinators made revisions, developing the checklist shown in Figure 2.2 (pp. 20–21). For the first year of implementation, they decided that component 2: selecting and stating objectives, component 3: explaining and modeling, and component 5: providing guided practice, were most important. (Note the asterisk on the checklist by these components, indicating that they are considered critical.) When collecting IC data and doing teacher observations, facilitators would focus most attention on these components. Jenkins and her associates identified variations within each component as ideal, acceptable, or unacceptable, to use as a guideline on which to base their expectations for the first year of implementation. (Note the use of the dotted and solid vertical lines on the checklist indicating ideal, acceptable, and unacceptable variations.) In the second year of implementation they would focus more attention on the remaining three components as well as on the initial three components identified as critical during the first year.

In late November, copies of the checklist were shared with all principals to communicate the district's expectations concerning implementation of the effective teaching program. The principals decided to meet with their teachers before the Christmas break, in departmental and grade-level meetings, to discuss the program and explain the district's expectations and priorities for the first year of implementation. Prior to this meeting, principals were encouraged to collect information about teacher concerns (more about this in chapter 3). Principals then structured their meetings around the concerns and issues raised by teachers. The principals reported that teachers found the meeting helpful and asked numerous questions about how much time they would have before they would be expected to begin using the program and how they would be evaluated on its use.

In January and February, instructional coordinators scheduled a series of grade-level and subject-area meetings focused on the specific components of the program identified as critical in year 1: selecting and stating objectives, explaining and modeling, and providing guided practice. In March and April, teachers were provided opportunities to observe "veteran" teachers using the program in a neighboring school district. A schedule was worked out in order to provide release time for each teacher who wanted to participate in this observation activity; substitutes were hired to cover the classes teachers missed while observing. In May, the principals and instructional coordinators completed an IC checklist on each teacher as one part of their assessment of the new program's first year of implementation.

Display and Interpretation of IC Data

Springdale School District's use of an IC component checklist demonstrates how IC can be used to help clarify a program in the initial

Figure 2.2. Springdale Effective Teaching Program Checklist

Component 1: Using an Anticipatory Set

(1)	(2)	(3)	(4)	(5)
Teacher typically uses an anticipatory set including the elements of review, preview, motivation, and direction	Teacher typically uses an anticipatory set that includes 1-2 appropriate elements	Teacher typically uses an anticipatory set that consists mainly of focusing attention	Teacher seldom uses an anticipatory set	Teacher never uses an anticipatory set

*Component 2: Selecting and Stating Objectives

(1)	(2)	(3)	(4)	(5)
Teacher typically uses an objective that is relevant to students and states it in student terms	Teacher typically uses an objective that is relevant to students but seldom states it	Teacher typically states objectives, but not in student terms	Teacher seldom uses an objective	Teacher never uses an objective

*Component 3: Explaining and Modeling

(1)	(2)	(3)	(4)
Teacher typically explains and models so that students see and understand	Teacher typically explains so that students understand but does not model	Teacher typically gives explanations that are not on the student's level	Teacher typically makes assignments with no explanation or modeling

Component 4: Checking for Understanding

(1)	(2)	(3)	(4)	(5)
Teacher typically checks for understanding and gives immediate feedback after each section of the lesson	Teacher occasionally checks for understanding and gives feedback during the lesson	Teacher typically checks for understanding at the end of the lesson and gives feedback	Teacher occasionally checks for understanding at the end of the lesson	Teacher typically assigns work without checking for understanding

*Component 5: Providing Guided Practice

(1)	(2)	(3)	(4)
Teacher typically checks work as students practice	Teacher occasionally checks work as students practice	Teacher does not check work as students practice	Teacher typically does not provide practice for students

*Component 6: Providing Independent Practice

(1)	(2)	(3)
Teacher typically assigns independent practice that is appropriate for all students in length and difficulty	Teacher typically assigns independent practice that is appropriate for most students, but inappropriate for a few	Teacher typically does not provide for independent practice

———— Variations to the right are unacceptable; variations to the left are acceptable.
- - - - - - Variations to the left are ideal, as prescribed by the developer.
*Denotes critical component
Note: This checklist is an integration of checklists focused on the Madalyn Hunter Effective Teaching Program developed by two North Carolina principals in the "Even Champions Have Coaches Training Program" (Draughon and Hord 1986).

phases of implementation. IC can also be helpful in monitoring an implementation effort in progress and in identifying innovation components that may need attention. Depending on the purpose for which the data are to be used, IC data can be organized and displayed in a number of ways. Two ways of organizing data that we have found to be especially useful are by individual user and by innovation component. Let's use the example of The Science Program (TSP) to demonstrate the utility of organizing data in these two ways (Hall, Hord, Rutherford, Loucks, Huling, and Heck 1982).

TSP is a second generation science curriculum based on the science curriculums developed in the '60s and the experiences of those who have used them over the years. TSP places equal emphasis on learning the basic principles and theories of science and learning to design, conduct, and interpret scientific investigations. The program emphasizes students' working with materials, with the teacher serving in a tutorial role. The program is divided into a series of units; each unit has a theme that gradually emerges as the activities of the unit are covered. A set of standardized TSP tests have been designed to assess achievement in science content and science process. The IC component checklist for TSP is shown in Figure 2.3.

To illustrate our approaches to organizing data, we will examine hypothetical IC data collected from ten teachers in the program midway through the first year of implementation. In Figure 2.4, the data from the ten teachers are displayed by individual user. These data indicate that Teacher D appears to be the farthest along in use of the program, while Teachers E and F show the least degree of implementation. Using this information, a facilitator might ask Teacher D to assist other teachers with their use of the program and investigate why Teachers E and F are not using the program more. The facilitator then can provide personalized assistance to help them improve their use of the program. The data also indicate that all teachers except Teachers A, B, and D could henefit from assistance in how to balance the content/process emphasis of the program, while Teachers B, E, and F need assistance focused on student grouping.

Organizing and displaying IC data by individual user helps to reveal what types of assistance would be most valuable to individual users. Also, with data organized this way, it is possible to identify individuals who are using identical or highly similar configurations of the program. For example, Teachers H and J are using the exact same configuration of the program; the configurations of Teachers G and I are also identical, and are highly similar to those of Teachers H and J. Teachers E and F have configurations highly similar to each other and probably could benefit from similar types of assistance. Additional insights can be gained by

Figure 2.3. (TSP) Science Program Configuration Checklist

*Component 1: Units Taught:

(1)	(2)	(3)	(4)	(5)
All units and most activities are taught	Most units and activities are taught	Some units are taught	A few selected activities are taught	No units or activities are taught

*Component 2: Use of Materials:

(1)	(2)	(3)
Students are constantly manipulating science materials	Only the teacher and selected students handle the materials most of the time	Typically, the teacher does demonstrations and the students watch

Component 3: Student Grouping:

(1)	(2)	(3)
Students work individually and in small groups	Students are kept in 3–5 permanent groups	The whole class is taught as a group

*Component 4: Process/Content Emphasis:

(1)	(2)	(3)	(4)
Science content and science processes are emphasized equally	Science content is given major emphasis	The processes of science are given major emphasis	Memorization of facts and reading about science are emphasized

*Component 5: Assessment:

(1)	(2)	(3)	(4)
All TSP assessment activities are used	Some TSP assessment activities are used	Teacher-made tests are used on a regular basis	Tests are not given regularly

_____ Variations to the right are unacceptable; variations to the left are acceptable.
- - - - - - Variations to the left are ideal, as prescribed by the developer.

*Denotes critical components.

Figure 2.4. Teachers Use of Each Component by Variation Numbers

Components

Teacher	1. Units Taught	2. Use of Materials	3. Student Grouping	4. Process/ Content Emphasis	5. Assessment
A	1	2	2	1	3
B	2	3	3	1	3
C	1	1	1	3	2
D	1	1	1	1	1
E	5	3	3	2	3
F	4	2	3	4	4
G	2	2	2	2	3
H	2	2	2	3	3
I	2	2	2	2	3
J	2	2	2	3	3

examining the IC data by innovation component, as shown in Figure 2.5. These data provide a more global overview of the implementation of TSP. The chart indicates that, considering the short time implementation has been under way, teacher use of the program is progressing well. Teachers are teaching many of the units and activities and, in some cases,

Figure 2.5. Percentage of Teachers Using Each Variation of Each Component

Component 1: Units Taught	1	2	3	4	5
	30%	50%		10%	10%

Component 2: Use of Materials	1	2	3
	20%	60%	20%

Component 3: Student Grouping	1	2	3
	20%	50%	30%

Component 4: Process/Content Emphasis	1	2	3	4
	30%	30%	30%	10%

Component 5: Assessment	1	2	3	4
	10%	10%	70%	10%

students are being allowed to manipulate the program materials. Teachers should be congratulated for their rapid progress with these aspects of the program. However, the IC data indicate some problems with the process/content emphasis of the program. There are also variations in how teachers are grouping students. The IC data, reorganized by innovation component, can provide insight into the parts of the program on which facilitators should focus. In this case, it appears that facilitators need to focus on helping teachers begin to use TSP tests and encourage the equal emphasis of content and process. The data indicate that using inservice sessions to reemphasize the use of units, activities, and materials probably would not be the best approach. Rather, Teachers E and F, who most need this type of assistance, should receive personalized attention.

Summary

In this chapter we have discussed the concept of Innovation Configurations (IC) and its application in school improvement. IC represents the different ways individual users implement an innovation in their own settings. It is important for you as a change facilitator to be able to identify the specific ways teachers are using a program so that you can make informed decisions about how to offer support and assistance. The concept of IC is particularly useful in helping to clarify and communicate expectations related to the use of an innovation during the initial implementation phase and in monitoring implementation in progress to identify the individuals and parts of the program that require the facilitator's attention.

The IC component checklist is a tool for summarizing the descriptions of identified component parts of an innovation and the variations in how parts are put to use. In some programs some components are considered critical while others are considered related. A critical component is one that must be used if the innovation is to be considered implemented, while a related component is not considered essential to the innovation, but is recommended by the developer or facilitator. Critical components are designated on the checklist with an asterisk (*).

A variety of IC component checklist formats can be used, but organizing the checklist in a left-to-right format, with the variations of each component organized across the page, has the advantage of graphically displaying those variations valued over others. The ideal or more acceptable variation of the component is displayed in the far left column, with the other variations ranging in order of descending acceptability across the page. Ideal or most acceptable practice is placed to the left of a dotted line; a solid vertical line is used to indicate unacceptable practice, placed to the right of the line. Variations located between the dotted and solid vertical lines are acceptable, though not ideal.

IC data can be displayed and used in a number of ways. Two particularly useful ways of organizing data are by individual user and by innovation component. When IC data are organized by individual user, it is possible to identify what types of assistance would be most valuable to specific persons. When IC data are organized by innovation component, it is possible to identify the parts of the program that are being used most successfully and those that require additional time and attention from the facilitator.

IC can be used for purposes of formative evaluation, to help pinpoint areas in need of attention, and to help facilitators decide how best to intervene. IC is also useful in summative evaluation; it addresses the question of how well a program has been implemented and thus helps evaluators decide how much confidence to place in the outcome data. If a program has been implemented to a high degree, facilitators usually can be confident that their outcome measures are a fair reflection of the program's success or failure. On the other hand, if the program has not been implemented acceptably, outcome data cannot fairly reflect a program's potential.

Innovation Configurations is a useful concept for change facilitators. Understanding how individuals are implementing a specific program provides you, the CF, with information for designing appropriate support and assistance. Used in combination with the other diagnostic dimensions of the Concerns-Based Adoption Model, Innovation Configurations can make a substantial difference in the school improvement process.

Frequently Asked Questions Related to IC

Q: *Is it better to collect IC data through observations or interviews?*

A: When collecting IC data, the more information the facilitator has the better. Ideally, the facilitator should visit with the teacher about the program several times and observe the teacher's classroom use of the program a number of times. We feel it is essential that an interview be conducted so that the facilitator can talk with the teacher about typical practice. A small number of observations is not sufficient to assess typical practice.

Q: *If an interview is used, how can you be sure the teacher will be truthful about his or her use of the program?*

A: The quality of IC data collected will depend on the rapport that the facilitator can establish with the teacher. The teacher must be made to feel that the facilitator honestly wants to be helpful, and that the visit is for purposes of collecting information about the program, not about the individual. A good place to start is for the facilitator to explain to the teacher that he or she is interested in the teacher's experience with the new program. The facilitator should then explain that the purpose of gathering information is to pinpoint where teachers stand with the program in order to be able to decide what types of assistance teachers will find most helpful. The focus should be on the innovation/program, not the teacher.

Q: *Can you ask teachers to complete their own IC component checklist in order to save the facilitator's time?*

A: That depends. When teachers are given a copy of an IC component checklist, they usually draw conclusions about what ideal or most acceptable practice should be even if it is not marked on the instrument. In this situation, it is difficult for teachers to indicate on the checklist that their practice is less than ideal, perhaps even unacceptable. For this reason, we strongly recommend that IC data be gathered via person-to-person discussion. On the other hand, if the CF has previously established a helping relationship with teachers and they understand the supportive nature of the instrument's use, reliable data may be obtained from a written questionnaire. If IC data are to be gathered through a paper-and-pencil measure, questions should be formulated so that teachers can respond freely about their typical classroom practice without feeling the pressure of having to compare their practice to an ideal standard. The facilitator could then complete the checklist using the information the teacher has provided.

3.
From the Teacher's Perspective

When Springdale's Julia Jenkins became aware of teacher uncertainties about how the program was to be used, she visited the schools and talked with teachers about the program. She was somewhat disappointed that most teachers did not comment more about how the program was serving students. Instead, the teachers had questions about whether written lesson plans were required and, if so, in what format, and when and how they would be evaluated in the teacher appraisal system. They were concerned about how to balance reteaching tasks with the need to cover all the objectives designated for their specific grade level or discipline.

A CENTRAL AND MAJOR PREMISE OF THE CBAM IS THAT THE SINGLE most important factor in any change process is the people who will be most affected by the change. Certainly, the innovation itself and the organization into which it is to be incorporated are important variables, but they are secondary in importance to the people who are the intended innovation users.

The importance of focusing on people can be seen in the Springdale situation. When Julia Jenkins visited schools to talk to teachers about the new effective teaching program, she was surprised and disappointed by the teachers' comments and questions. The teachers expressed personal or self-concerns (how would they be evaluated) and task, or management, concerns (balancing reteaching with the need to cover all objectives). Informational concerns were also voiced (we need to know what is expected of us regarding lesson plans).

Jenkins was disappointed because she expected the teachers to talk to her about the effects or impact of innovation on students, and they did not do so.

At this point, a tempting option for Jenkins might be to try to "correct" the problem she perceives by recommending additional inservice training for teachers. Suppose that additional inservice is planned, and it is designed to emphasize how effective the innovation has been in other school districts and how it can be equally effective in the Springdale schools. Teachers might also be encouraged to find ways to evaluate the effects of the program on students. How do you think the teachers will respond to this type of inservice delivered at this time, just several months into the implementation effort? Our answer to this question is presented in this chapter.

Vividly reflected in this illustration from Springdale is the fact that when engaged in any change process, teachers will have specific and individualistic concerns about the change and their involvement in it. Concerns refer to the feelings, thoughts, and reactions individuals have about a new program or innovation that touches their lives. Being concerned about change is universal, even though the nature of the concerns varies from person to person. Concerns exert a powerful influence on the implementation of a change, and they determine the kinds of assistance that teachers find useful.

Stages of Concern

The Stages of Concern (SoC) dimension of the CBAM focuses on the concerns of individuals involved in change (Hall 1979). Research has identified seven kinds of concerns that users, or potential users, of an innovation may have. These concerns are organized in the model as Stages of Concern (Figure 3.1). While the seven Stages of Concern are distinctive, they are not mutually exclusive. An individual is likely to have some degree of concern at all stages at any given time, yet our studies have documented that the stage or stages where concerns are more (and less) intense will vary as the implementation of change progresses. These variations in intensity mark the developmental nature of individual concerns. The developmental nature of concerns is further reflected in the three dimensions—self, task, and impact—into which the seven stages may be grouped (Figure 3.1).

Figure 3.1. Stages of Concern: Typical Expressions of Concern about the Innovation

	Stages of Concern	Expressions of Concern
I M P A C T	6 Refocusing	I have some ideas about something that would work even better.
	5 Collaboration	I am concerned about relating what I am doing with what other instructors are doing.
	4 Consequence	How is my use affecting kids?
T A S K	3 Management	I seem to be spending all my time getting material ready.
S E L F	2 Personal	How will using it affect me?
	1 Informational	I would like to know more about it.
	0 Awareness	I am not concerned about it (the innovation).

When a change effort is in its early stages, teachers are very likely to have *self-concerns* (stage 1, informational; stage 2, personal). They will want to know more about the innovation—what it is and how it is similar to and different from what they already are doing. Teachers may also want to know when the new program will begin, the kind of preparation they will receive, the source of the new program, who is endorsing it and why, and how it is supposed to work.

Personal concerns are also likely to be intense during this time, although they may not be expressed as openly as informational concerns. The teachers who asked Julia Jenkins how they would be evaluated in the new program were expressing personal concerns. Teachers may also be concerned about their ability to execute the new program as expected and about making mistakes that would make them look foolish. Another way teachers express personal concerns about a change is to characterize the innovation as nothing new, but as something they have always done or used to do. With this conviction, they may convince themselves they really do not have to change.

Task concerns (stage 3, management) typically become more intense as final preparations are made for beginning use of an innovation and during the early period of use. Jenkins's teachers who wanted to know how to balance the need to reteach with the need to cover all objectives were expressing management concerns—how do we get the time to do this, and how do we arrange to have different students doing different things at the same time? Expressions related to the management of time are common when concerns at this stage are intense. Teachers who say they are staying just one day ahead of the students or that they are having problems getting necessary teaching materials ready and organized are also expressing management concerns.

When teachers' most intense concerns are about the effects of an innovation on students and what can be done to improve the effectiveness of the program, they have reached the impact level. Stages 4 (consequence), 5 (collaboration), and 6 (refocusing) compose the impact dimension. Many teachers will never have intense concerns at stages 5 or 6. Stage 5 pertains to concerns about collaborating with others to improve the outcomes of an innovation, and for those teachers who have no opportunity or need for collaboration this concern may never emerge. When teachers have used an innovation with efficiency for some time they may become concerned about finding even better ways to reach and teach students. Only a few teachers have these types of concerns, but when they do, these concerns are indicative of stage 6 (refocusing).

Developmental Nature of Concerns

While concerns about a change typically progress through the stages in a developmental manner, the progression is not absolute and certainly does not happen to each person in a like manner. Everyone will not move through the stages at the same pace nor have the same intensity of concern at the various stages. It is most probable that concerns will develop in a wave pattern. That is, self-concerns will be most intense early in the change process and abate with time, and task or management concerns will rise. Only after management concerns have been reduced in intensity can impact concerns be expected to intensify. The pattern and intensity of concerns people experience during a period of change are directly affected by the nature of the change and the kind and, especially, the amount of assistance provided. The effective teaching program being implemented in the Springdale schools might be considered a complex innovation. As noted in chapter 2, the program has several components, and many teachers will be required to make a number of changes in their classroom procedures. This innovation will affect concerns more markedly than would a simpler change that would have little or no direct effect on teaching practices. The more complex an innovation, the greater the need for skilled facilitation of the change, facilitation that carefully attends to the concerns of teachers. More will be said later about facilitating change.

Procedures for Assessing Concerns

Three procedures may be used to determine concerns. The most practical is face-to-face conversation. This works best if the conversation is an informal talk rather than a formal, scheduled conference. During the conversation, the facilitator should ask questions that stimulate the teacher to express feelings and concerns. In the Springdale district, a useful question would be, "How are you feeling about the teaching effectiveness program?" Or you might ask for reactions to specific aspects of the program, such as the new approach to planning or the step-by-step procedure for teaching. Responses to each of these questions may cue additional questions.

Asking appropriate questions in an informal, relaxed manner is the first key to successfully using one-to-one conversations. A second requirement is that the questioner be a good listener, and this means several things: after asking a question, allow respondents time to say all they wish without interruption; do not try to direct the responses or to "put words in their mouths"; give respondents evidence that you really are listening (this can be done by asking elaborative questions or by restating certain statements to ensure clarity of understanding); finally, listen to the whole response and try to avoid selective listening.

A third requirement in this procedure is to be able to analyze the content of the response for the concerns being expressed. When analyzing the content, be sure to consider the entire response, not just part of it. Suppose a teacher states, "The program is not working very well with my classes because I just don't have time to develop the materials I need." The first portion of the statement might indicate that the teacher is expressing concerns about the impact of the program on students (stage 4, consequence). When the second portion of the statement is considered, however, it becomes apparent that the teacher's concerns are really focused on time and materials (stage 3, management).

A second procedure that can be used for determining concerns is the open-ended statement (Newlove and Hall 1976). This procedure is more formal than the conversational approach described above and is not ordinarily used with one person. It is more appropriate for soliciting information from groups. With this technique, individuals are asked to write complete sentences to answer a question such as, "When you think about _____, what are you concerned about?" In the Springdale district, "the effective teaching program" could be inserted in the blank, or any other phrases representing areas in which the facilitator may wish to gain information. Respondents should be encouraged to answer in complete sentences so as to provide enough information for accurate analysis. As a rule, brevity of response is not a problem, in fact it is not uncommon to get paragraphs.

When analyzing written statements, we recommend that each sentence be considered separately (when there is more than one sentence) and then that all sentences be considered collectively. The following examples offer a guide to analyzing open-ended statements.

(1) Almost every night I wonder if I'll be able to locate and organize the material I will be using the next day. (2) I can't yet prevent surprises that cause a lot of wasted time. (3) I am not yet able to anticipate what things I will need to requisition for next week.

Sentence 1 indicates the teacher's concern about materials and their organization, which are management concerns (stage 3). Concern about wasted time (sentence 2) is another expression of management concerns. Finally, sentence 3 also reflects management concerns. Collectively, these sentences show that this person's greatest concern is managing the innovation. Pinpointing concerns is not always so clear cut, as can be seen in the following paragraph.

(1) I seem to spend most of my time giving and scoring the criterion tests. (2) I would like to observe some other teachers to see how they handle this problem. (3) At times I feel that I must be a poor teacher.

Management of time (stage 3) is clearly the concern expressed in the first sentence. In the second sentence the teacher is asking for more information (stage 1) that would respond to that management concern. The third sentence is an expression of personal concern (stage 2). In cases like this, when more than one stage of concern is expressed, the collective analysis is straightforward: the individual's greatest concerns are at stages 1, 2, and 3. Do not average stages 1, 2, and 3 to arrive at a single average stage.

Several notes of caution should be heeded when using either one-to-one conferences or open-ended statements. In both cases, people will express only those feelings that are of greatest concern to them. They will also have concerns at the other stages, even though not expressed, and this should not be ignored when responding to their concerns. Secondly, both procedures provide only limited information upon which to base a determination. While the procedures are reliable enough for clinical work, they should not be considered infallible or used for research or evaluation. In addition, information obtained through routine interactions with teachers may be used to enrich these data. Finally, remember that concerns are not fixed; they do change, so they should be periodically reassessed.

A third procedure for assessing concerns is the Stages of Concern Questionnaire (SoCQ) (Hall, George, and Rutherford 1979). The SoCQ is a 35-item paper-and-pencil measure that typically requires only 10–15 minutes to complete. Scoring can be done by hand or via computer. (An example of the SoCQ and the hand-scoring instrument are included at the end of this chapter.) Because of its formal nature, the SoCQ is most often used with groups when research or program evaluation is being conducted, but a facilitator certainly can use it to assess the concerns of a school faculty or another subgroup within the school. Julia Jenkins could have used it to get a clear picture of the concerns of Springdale teachers about the effective teaching program.

The SoCQ has several strengths. One is its accuracy of assessment. The instrument was developed through extensive research that has assured its validity and reliability. Beyond that, it identifies concerns by quantitative scores for each stage, eliminating the need for inferring concerns from verbal or written statements. A second major strength of the questionnaire is the completeness of the data it provides. For each individual, a profile is developed (this can be done by computer or by hand). This profile shows the intensity level on each of the seven stages, thereby presenting a useful pattern of concerns (see Figure 3.2). When a facilitator is using concerns as a guide to action, it may be useful to know a person's low, mid-range, and most intense concerns.

Another strength of the SoCQ is its versatility. It can be reliably administered to the same persons several times during the course of a year. When this is done, a profile can be computer generated that not only shows current concerns but any changes that have occurred in the pattern of concerns from one administration to the next. For the facilitator who is targeting assistance in response to concerns, this pattern of changes offers insights into the effectiveness of those actions.

Profiles for groups, rather than individuals, also can be developed from the SoCQ. As is always the case when developing group averages, individual differences are screened out, but there are still times when a group profile can be useful. For example, Jenkins could find it very useful to have a concerns profile for each school in the Springdale district.

Interpreting Concerns

When learning and trying to apply anything new, there is no substitute for experience and training. So it is with concerns and other components of the CBAM model. The information presented here is intended to launch you on a journey toward excellence through understanding and addressing concerns, but special training may be necessary to use Stages of Concern to their full potential.

Several profiles resulting from the SoCQ are presented below and discussed. Skill in analyzing SoCQ profiles is valuable in and of itself, but it also greatly enriches one's skill in understanding information gained from one-to-one conversation and open-ended concerns statements.

Probably the most readily identified and commonly found concerns profile is that of the nonuser, the individual who has not begun using an innovation. In the research that has been done to date using the Stages of Concern Questionnaire, the nonuser concerns profile stands out most clearly and consistently. Nonusers' concerns are normally highest on stages 0, 1, and 2, and lowest on stages 4, 5, and 6. There is some variation in the intensity of these concerns depending on the innovation

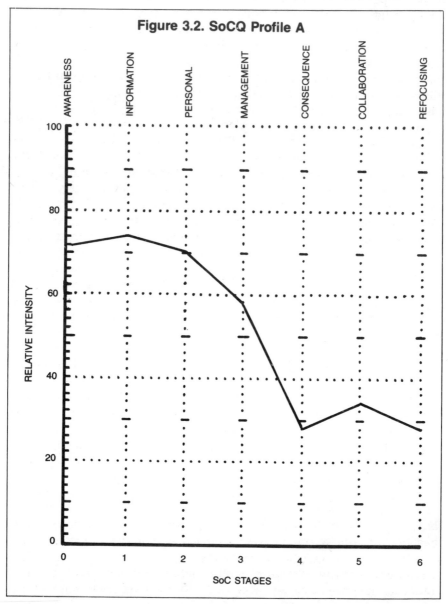

Figure 3.2. SoCQ Profile A

and the setting where it is being implemented, but the general shape of the pattern is plotted in Figure 3.2.

The profile illustrated in Figure 3.2 is that of an interested person who is somewhat aware of and concerned about the innovation (stage 0) and is interested in learning more about the innovation from a positive, proactive perspective (stage 1 slightly higher than stage 2). The person does not have a great deal of management concern (medium intensity stage 3) and is not intensely concerned about the innovation's consequences for students (low stages 4 and 5). The low, tailing-off stage 6 score suggests that the person does not have other ideas that would compete with the innovation. The overall profile reflects a person who wants additional information about the innovation but also has some fairly intense personal concerns about its potential use.

In contrast to the first profile, Figure 3.3 depicts various degrees of doubt and potential resistance to the innovation. This can be clearly identified in what is referred to as the "one/two split." When stage 2 concerns are equal to or more intense than the stage 1 concerns, the innovation is perceived much differently than in the previous illustration. In general, when such a "negative one/two split" occurs, personal concerns (stage 2) override concerns about learning more about the innovation (stage 1). The individual is much more concerned about personal well-being in relation to the change than about learning more of a substantive nature about the innovation. For individuals in this situation, stage 2 concerns normally have to be reduced before they can look at a proposed innovation objectively and begin to receive and use information about it.

Single-Peak Profiles

The most common concerns profiles have a single peak at either stage 3, 4, 5, or 6. People with such profiles are almost always involved in using the innovation. In general, profile interpretations can be based heavily upon the definition of the stage that has the highest score. In many cases, the second highest score will be quite a bit lower than the highest stage score. If the second highest score is more than 20 percentile points below the highest, it normally does not account for many of the intense concerns of the respondent. If certain stage scores are dramatically low, they indicate areas where people are reporting minimal or no concerns.

In Figure 3.4, for example, management (stage 3) concerns are relatively intense. The respondent is indicating high concern about time, logistics, or other managerial problems related to the innovation. The respondent is also somewhat concerned about the consequences of the innovation (stage 4), but not concerned about working with others (low stage 5). No intense personal concerns about the innovation (low stage 2) are evident.

Multiple-Peak Profiles

Multiple-peak profiles are not easy to interpret, but some combinations are reasonably straightforward. Figure 3.5 presents one of these

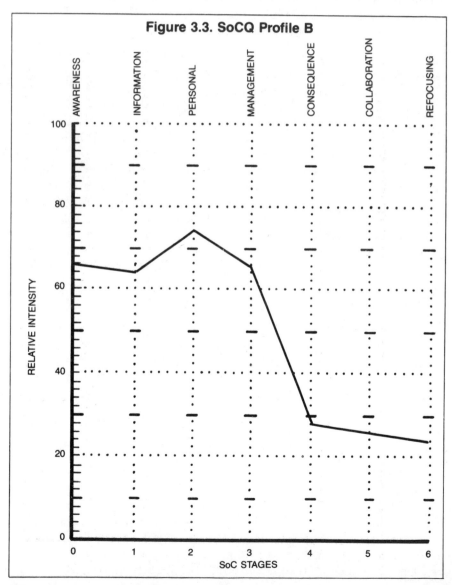

Figure 3.3. SoCQ Profile B

combinations: high concerns on stage 3 (management) and stage 6 (refocusing). This kind of profile signals the need for immediate attention by the change facilitator. The high stage 3 concerns indicate the person is having difficulty doing what is required by the innovation. High refocusing concerns (stage 6) indicate the person has ideas about improvements on the innovation. Most often, what the person thinks would be better is a return to old practices. Unless something changes,

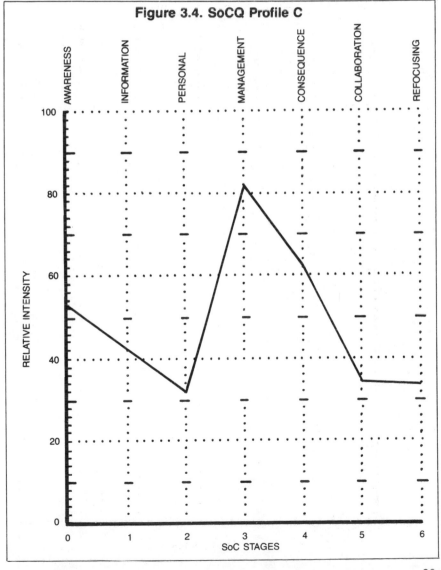

Figure 3.4. SoCQ Profile C

this person will probably abandon the innovation and go back to more comfortable old practices.

Two other multiple-peak profiles that occur with some frequency are seen in Figures 3.6 and 3.7. The person represented in Figure 3.6 also has high management concerns (stage 3), but these are accompanied by high informational concerns (stage 1). This person is probably in search

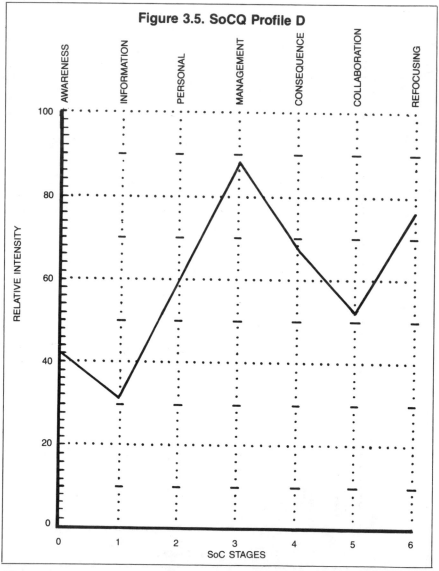

Figure 3.5. SoCQ Profile D

of information that will aid in managing the innovation and making it work more efficiently.

Figure 3.7 reflects a person who is concerned about how the innovation is affecting students (high consequence concerns). The low intensity of concerns on stages 2 and 3 suggests this person feels secure in using the innovation. This person also has high refocusing concerns (stage 6),

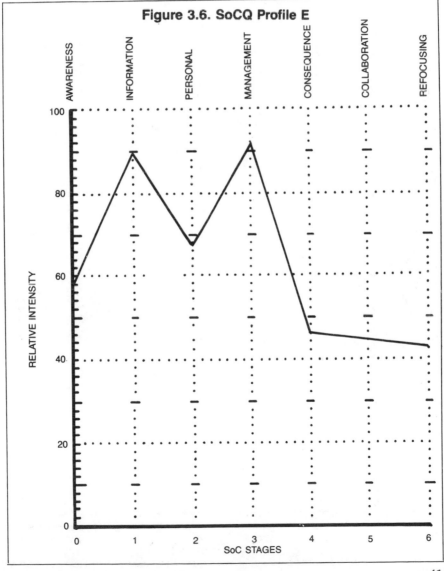

Figure 3.6. SoCQ Profile E

but when these are coupled with high consequence concerns, the major concerns are usually about making changes that will benefit students rather than making changes to make teaching life easier (as is the case for the person represented in Figure 3.5).

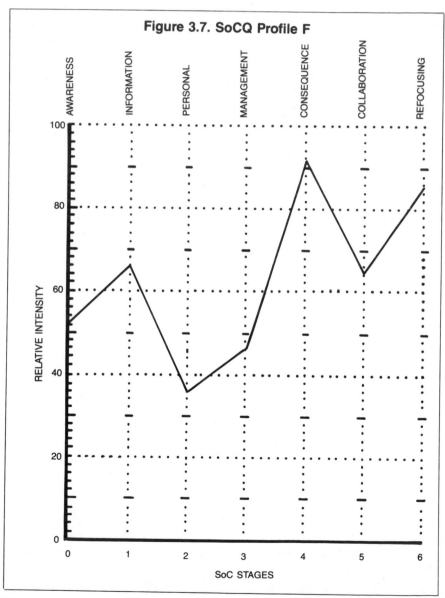

Figure 3.7. SoCQ Profile F

General Principles of Concerns

Concerns can be a highly effective guide to actions that school leaders or others might take to facilitate the implementation of change. Before offering specific suggestions of how this might be done, it is necessary to establish some general principles.

There is nothing inherently good or bad about a particular stage or pattern of concerns. As an analogy, a chronological age of 16 years is not necessarily better or worse than an age of 6 or 26. But we do not interact with a teenager in the same way as with a 6- or 26-year-old. So it should be with concerns. Our interactions with a person who has high personal concerns may be quite different from those with someone with high consequence concerns, but neither person or Stage of Concern is better or worse than the other.

The developmental and interactive nature of concerns is real and must not be ignored. For example, individuals who have high personal concerns will have little or no receptivity to assistance that is directed toward management or impact concerns unless they find in that kind of assistance something that responds to their personal concerns. In Springdale, had Julia Jenkins arranged for inservice training that focused on the impact of the innovation for teachers who had task and self-concerns, it would have been of little or no value. In fact, that kind of inservice could intensify personal concerns by confronting teachers with increased expectations. Once personal concerns have been reduced, it is highly probable management concerns will become the highest. Only after these management concerns are reduced will impact concerns elevate, although it is possible, but rare, that one could move from self-concerns to impact concerns.

Movement through the stages of concern cannot be forced, but, with appropriate support and assistance, it can be aided. At the same time, a lack of assistance or the wrong kind of support can interfere with developmental changes in concerns. Concerns are not fixed. In addition to changing developmentally, they will recycle in response to each new innovation or even to phases of an incremental innovation. However, an individual's pattern of concerns in relation to one innovation may vary greatly from the same person's pattern regarding another innovation.

Concerns do not exist in a vacuum. Concerns are influenced by participants' feelings about an innovation, by their perception of their ability to use it, by the setting in which the change occurs, by the number of other changes in which they are involved and, most of all, by the kind of support and assistance they receive as they attempt to implement change.

Concerns and the Facilitation of Change

A first step in using concerns to guide interventions is to know what concerns the individuals have, especially their most intense concerns. The second step is to deliver interventions that might respond to those concerns. Unfortunately, there is no absolute set of universal prescriptions, but the following suggestions offer examples of interventions that might be useful.

Stage 0—Awareness Concerns
   a. If possible, involve teachers in discussions and decisions about the innovation and its implementation.
   b. Share enough information to arouse interest, but not so much that it overwhelms.
   c. Acknowledge that a lack of awareness is expected and reasonable, and that no questions about the innovation are foolish.
   d. Encourage unaware persons to talk with colleagues who know about the innovation.
   e. Take steps to minimize gossip and inaccurate sharing of information about the innovation.

Stage 1—Informational Concerns
   a. Provide clear and accurate information about the innovation.
   b. Use a variety of ways to share information—verbally, in writing, and through any available media. Communicate with individuals and with small and large groups.
   c. Have persons who have used the innovation in other settings visit with your teachers. Visits to user schools could also be arranged.
   d. Help teachers see how the innovation relates to their current practices, both in regard to similarities and differences.
   e. Be enthusiastic and enhance the visibility of others who are excited.

Stage 2—Personal Concerns
   a. Legitimize the existence and expression of personal concerns. Knowing these concerns are common and that others have them can be comforting.
   b. Use personal notes and conversations to provide encouragement and reinforce personal adequacy.
   c. Connect these teachers with others whose personal concerns have diminished and who will be supportive.
   d. Show how the innovation can be implemented sequentially rather than in one big leap. It is important to establish expectations that

are attainable.

e. Do not push innovation use, but encourage and support it while maintaining expectations.

Stage 3—Management Concerns

a. Clarify the steps and components of the innovation. Information from innovation configurations will be helpful here.

b. Provide answers that address the small specific "how-to" issues that are so often the cause of management concerns.

c. Demonstrate exact and practical solutions to the logistical problems that contribute to these concerns.

d. Help teachers sequence specific activities and set timelines for their accomplishments.

e. Attend to the immediate demands of the innovation, not what will be or could be in the future.

Stage 4—Consequence Concerns

a. Provide these individuals with opportunities to visit other settings where the innovation is in use and to attend conferences on the topic.

b. Don't overlook these individuals. Give them positive feedback and needed support.

c. Find opportunities for these persons to share their skills with others.

d. Share with these persons information pertaining to the innovation.

Stage 5—Collaboration Concerns

a. Provide these individuals with opportunities to develop those skills necessary for working collaboratively.

b. Bring together those persons, both within and outside the school, who are interested in collaboration.

c. Help the collaborators establish reasonable expectations and guidelines for the collaborative effort.

d. Use these persons to provide technical assistance to others who need assistance.

e. Encourage the collaborators, but don't attempt to force collaboration on those who are not interested.

Stage 6—Refocusing Concerns

a. Respect and encourage the interest these persons have for finding a better way.

b. Help these individuals channel their ideas and energies in ways that will be productive rather than counterproductive.

    c. Encourage these individuals to act on their concerns for program improvement.

    d. Help these persons access the resources they may need to refine their ideas and put them into practice.

    e. Be aware of and willing to accept the fact the these persons may replace or significantly modify the existing innovations.

    Individuals do have concerns about change, and these concerns will have a powerful influence on the implementation of change. The CBAM offers several easy ways to identify these concerns. It is up to those who guide change to identify concerns, interpret them, and then act on them.

Questions Often Asked about Concerns

    Q: *Is it possible that a person of a particular "personality type" is likely to remain at one particular stage?*

    A: This is highly unlikely. The nature of an innovation and the demands it places on users have a much greater influence on individuals than does their personality type. Personality type may influence the intensity of people's concerns but will not prevent them from experiencing the typical Stages of Concern.

    Q: *Is SoC linear or cyclic?*

    A: With regard to a specific innovation, individuals will typically move through the stages in a linear manner, at least up to a point. For example, many users never have intense concerns about collaboration and refocusing. It is not uncommon, however, for concerns to recycle to some extent. For example, individuals with high management concerns that go unresolved may develop intense personal concerns. Concerns will recycle, of course, with each innovation.

    Q: *Is it valid to assume a person "wants to move" to a higher Stage of Concern?*

    A: No it isn't. One of the responsibilities of a facilitator is to arouse higher Stages of Concern while responding to existing stages. For example, individuals at the awareness stage may never have informational concerns unless something is done to prompt them. Individuals who have intense concerns at stage 2 (personal) or stage 3 (management) will be uncomfortable with an innovation and want to change their situation, but they could do this by ignoring the innovation and not being concerned about it. Effective facilitators are needed to help these people resolve their concerns and advance to consequence concerns.

Q: *How can I get the SoCQ?*

A: The questionnaire is included here, beginning on the following page. It is also found in the *Manual for the Use of the SoC Questionnaire*. The citation for this manual, (Hall, George, and Rutherford 1979) can be found in the list of references at the end of this book. Information about the manual may be obtained from the Southwest Educational Development Laboratory as noted at the beginning of the reference list.

Directions for Using the SoCQ Quick Scoring Device

Developed by Eddie W. Parker and Teresa H. Griffin

The Stages of Concern Questionnaire (SoCQ), on pages 48-49, contains 35 items. The scoring of the SoCQ requires a series of operations which result in an SoCQ profile.

Instructions

The following steps have been carried out on the attached Quick Scoring Device, pages 50-51, for subject number 0001, using this subject's responses on the SoCQ.

Step 1: In the box labeled *A*, fill in the identifying information taken from the cover sheet of the SoC Questionnaire.

Step 2: Copy the numerical values of the circled responses to statements 1 through 18 in the numbered blanks in the Table labeled *B*. Note that the numbered blanks in Table *B* are *not* in consecutive order.

Step 3: Box *C* contains the Raw Scale Score Total for each stage (0–6). Take each of the seven columns (0–6) in Table *B*, add the numbers within each column, and enter the sum for each column (0–6) in the appropriate blank in Box *C*. Each of these seven Raw Score Totals is a number between 0 and 35.

SoCQ Quick Scoring Device

A. Identifying Information	B. Raw Scale Scores (35 Items)

D. Percentile Table	C. Raw Score Totals (Stages 0–6)
	E. Percentile Scores (Stages 0–6)
	F. SoC Profile

Step 4: Table *D* contains the percentile scores for each Stage of Concern. Find the Raw Scale Score Total for Stage 0 from Box *C* ("5" in the example); locate this number ("5") in the left-hand column in Table *D*, then look in the Stage 0 column to the right in Table *D* and circle that percentile ranking ("53" in the example). Do the same for Stages 1 through 6.

Step 5: Transcribe the circled percentile scores for each stage (0–6) from Table *D* to Box *E*. Box *E* now contains seven numbers between 0 and 99.

Step 6: Box *F* contains the SoC graph. From Box *E*, take the percentile score for Stage 0 ("53" in the example) and mark that point with a dot on the Stage 0 vertical line on the SoC graph. Do the same for Stages 1 through 6. Connect the points to form the SoC profile.

For interpretation of the SoC profile, refer to Hall, George, and Rutherford (1979), The SoCQ Manual.

Concerns Questionnaire

Name _____

In order to identify these data, please give us the last four digits of your Social Security number:

_____   _____   _____   _____

The purpose of this questionnaire is to determine what people who are using or thinking about using various programs are concerned about at various times during the innovation adoption process. The items were developed from typical responses of school and college teachers who ranged from no knowledge at all about various programs to many years experience in using them. Therefore, *a good part of the items on this questionnaire may appear to be of little relevance or irrelevant to you at this time*. For the completely irrelevant items, please circle "0" on the scale. Other items will represent those concerns you *do* have, in varying degrees of intensity, and should be marked higher on the scale. For example:

This statement is very true of me at this time.	0	1	2	3	4	5	6	7
This statement is somewhat true of me now.	0	1	2	3	4	5	6	7
This statement is not at all true of of me at this time.	0	1	2	3	4	5	6	7
This statement seems irrelevant to me.	0	1	2	3	4	5	6	7

Please respond to the items in terms of *your present concerns*, or how you feel about your involvement or potential involvement with _____ (please specify the innovation. We do not hold to any one definition of this program, so please think of it in terms of *your own perceptions* of what it involves. Remember to respond to each item in terms of *your present concerns* about your involvement or potential involvement with the above named innovation.

Thank you for taking time to complete this task.

* * *

0	1	2	3	4	5	6	7
irrelevant	Not true of me now			Somewhat true of me now		Very true	

1. I am concerned about students' attitudes toward this innovation.	0	1	2	3	4	5	6	7
2. I now know of some other approaches that might work better.	0	1	2	3	4	5	6	7
3. I don't even know what the innovation is.	0	1	2	3	4	5	6	7
4. I am concerned about not having enough time to organize myself each day.	0	1	2	3	4	5	6	7
5. I would like to help other faculty in their use of the innovation.	0	1	2	3	4	5	6	7
6. I have a very limited knowledge about the innovation.	0	1	2	3	4	5	6	7
7. I would like to know the effect of reorganization on my professional status.	0	1	2	3	4	5	6	7
8. I am concerned about conflict between my interests and my responsibilities.	0	1	2	3	4	5	6	7
9. I am concerned about revising my use of the innovation.	0	1	2	3	4	5	6	7
10. I would like to develop working relationships with both our faculty and outside faculty using this innovation.	0	1	2	3	4	5	6	7
11. I am concerned about how the innovation affects students.	0	1	2	3	4	5	6	7
12. I am not concerned about this innovation.	0	1	2	3	4	5	6	7

13. I would like to know who will make the decisions in the new system.   0 1 2 3 4 5 6 7

14. I would like to discuss the possibility of using the innovation.   0 1 2 3 4 5 6 7

15. I would like to know what resources are available if we decide to adopt this innovation.   0 1 2 3 4 5 6 7

16. I am concerned about my inability to manage all the innovation requires.   0 1 2 3 4 5 6 7

17. I would like to know how my teaching or administration is supposed to change.   0 1 2 3 4 5 6 7

18. I would like to familiarize other departments or persons with the progress of this new approach.   0 1 2 3 4 5 6 7

19. I am concerned about evaluating my impact on students.   0 1 2 3 4 5 6 7

20. I would like to revise the innovation's instructional approach.   0 1 2 3 4 5 6 7

21. I am completely occupied with other things.   0 1 2 3 4 5 6 7

22. I would like to modify our use of the innovation based on the experiences of our students.   0 1 2 3 4 5 6 7

23. Although I don't know about this innovation, I am concerned about things in the area.   0 1 2 3 4 5 6 7

24. I would like to excite my students about their part in this approach.   0 1 2 3 4 5 6 7

25. I am concerned about time spent working with nonacademic problems related to this innovation.   0 1 2 3 4 5 6 7

26. I would like to know what the use of the innovation will require in the immediate future.   0 1 2 3 4 5 6 7

27. I would like to coordinate my effort with others to maximize the innovation's effects.   0 1 2 3 4 5 6 7

28. I would like to have more information on time and energy commitments required by this innovation.   0 1 2 3 4 5 6 7

29. I would like to know what other faculty are doing in this area.   0 1 2 3 4 5 6 7

30. At this time, I am not interested in learning about this innovation.   0 1 2 3 4 5 6 7

31. I would like to determine how to supplement, enhance, or replace the innovation.   0 1 2 3 4 5 6 7

32. I would like to use feedback from students to change the program.   0 1 2 3 4 5 6 7

33. I would like to know how my role will change when I am using the innovation.   0 1 2 3 4 5 6 7

34. Coordination of tasks and people is taking too much of my time.   0 1 2 3 4 5 6 7

35. I would like to know how this innovation is better than what we have now.   0 1 2 3 4 5 6 7

Copyright 1974. Procedures for Adopting Educational Innovations/CBAM Project, R&D Center for Teacher Education, University of Texas at Austin.

SoCQ Quick Scoring Device

A

Date: _9-18-78_

Site: _Austin_   SSN: _0001_

Innovation: _Bilingual Education_

D

Five Item Raw Scale Score Total	Percentiles for						
	Stage 0	Stage 1	Stage 2	Stage 3	Stage 4	Stage 5	Stage 6
0	10	5	5	2	1	1	1
1	23	12	12	5	1	2	2
2	29	16	14	7	1	3	3
3	37	19	17	9	2	3	5
4	46	23	21	11	2	4	6
5	(53)	27	25	15	3	5	9
6	60	30	28	18	3	7	11
7	66	34	31	23	4	9	14
8	72	37	35	27	5	10	17
9	77	40	39	30	5	12	20
10	81	43	41	34	7	14	22
11	84	45	45	39	8	16	26
12	86	48	48	43	9	19	30
13	89	51	52	47	11	22	34
14	91	54	55	52	13	25	38
15	93	57	57	56	16	28	42
16	94	60	59	60	19	31	47
17	95	63	63	65	21	36	52
18	96	66	67	69	24	40	57
19	97	69	70	73	27	44	60
20	98	72	72	77	30	48	65
21	98	(75)	76	80	33	52	69
22	99	80	78	83	(38)	55	73
23	99	84	80	85	43	59	77
24	99	88	83	88	48	64	81
25	99	90	85	98	54	68	(84)
26	99	91	(87)	(92)	59	72	87
27	99	93	89	94	63	76	90
28	99	95	91	95	66	80	92
29	99	96	92	97	71	84	94
30	99	97	94	97	76	88	96
31	99	98	95	98	82	(91)	97
32	99	99	96	98	86	93	98
33	99	99	96	99	90	95	99
34	99	99	97	99	92	97	99
35	99	99	99	99	96	98	99

B

	0		1		2		3		4		5		6
3	0	6	1	7	5	4	4	1	3	5	7	2	2
12	1	14	5	13	4	8	6	11	5	10	6	9	6
21	1	15	5	17	6	16	5	19	4	18	6	20	5
23	2	26	6	28	5	25	6	24	4	27	6	22	6
30	1	35	4	33	6	34	5	32	6	29	6	31	6

C

5	21	26	26	22	31	25

0	1	2	3	4	5	6

E

53	75	87	92	38	91	84

F

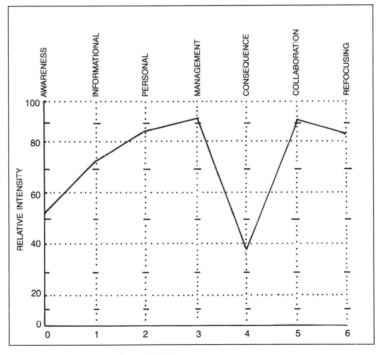

SoC STAGES

Copyright 1978

4.
Use of an Innovation in Classrooms

By the spring of the first year of use of the effective teaching program, Julia Jenkins was pleased with its progress. Through development and use of the Innovation Configuration checklist, she found it easier to communicate what the program entails and to pinpoint variations in its use. Through a series of sessions with the principals and the central office instructional staff, expectations for use of the program were becoming more clear and consistent. In turn, facilitators were working closely with teachers to help resolve their initial information, personal, and management concerns.

Jenkins had noted that although the implementation process was generally going well, there was noticeable variation in the way individual teachers were using the program. And the variations appeared to occur among schools as well.

Jenkins wanted to give the school board a first-year progress report. At the same time, she wanted to educate board members as to why it would probably take longer than a year before the district would realize the desired improvement in achievement scores. For this progress report she decided that, in addition to the information she had about "configurations" of the program and teacher concerns, she would also need to collect and report data on Levels of Use, a third CBAM diagnostic tool.

Taking Charge of Change

SPRINGDALE'S JULIA JENKINS WAS MORE ASTUTE THAN MANY INI-
tiators and facilitators of change. She saw the need to know how the
innovation was actually being used in classrooms. One of the most
common and serious mistakes administrators and change facilitators
make is to presume that once an innovation has been introduced and
initial training has been completed, the intended users will put it into
practice. Unfortunately, implementing an innovation is seldom so simple.

In school after school where changes have been introduced, research has shown that there are people who do not use the innovation at
all, even months or years after the introduction. There are others who
use only parts of an innovation, while still others try to use it but
struggle. Since changes are introduced into organizations for the express
purpose of bringing about improvement, who would expect improvement to occur if innovations are not used or are used ineffectively? Of
course no one would expect improvement under those conditions, but
time after time organizations will seek to assess the effectiveness of an
innovation without ever examining how it is being used. As a result,
innovation after innovation judged in this way has been discarded (or
deemphasized) because it did not produce the expected outcomes.

A prime responsibility of change facilitators is to guide the change
process to a point of successful implementation. To accomplish this, the
facilitator must monitor how an innovation is being used and act upon
that information. The CBAM offers administrators and facilitators a
proven technique for innovation monitoring—the assessment of Levels
of Use (Hall, Loucks, Rutherford, and Newlove 1975). The Levels of Use
(LoU) dimension describes the behaviors of the users of an innovation
through various stages—from spending most efforts in orienting, to
managing, and finally to integrating use of the innovation. Before use
actually begins, the individual becomes familiar with and increasingly
knowledgeable about the innovation. Initial use is typically disjointed,
and management problems are quite common. With continued use
management becomes routine, and the user is able to direct more effort
toward increased effectiveness for the learners and integrate what he or
she is doing with what others are doing. Experience is essential but not
sufficient to ensure that a given individual will develop high-quality use
of an innovation; appropriate support and assistance are also needed.

It should be noted that the LoU dimension describes behaviors of
innovation users and does not at all focus on attitudinal, motivational, or
other affective aspects of the user. LoU does not attempt to explain
causality. Instead, the LoU dimension is an attempt to define opera-
tionally what the user is doing.

Eight distinct Levels of Use have been identified (Figure 4.1). Each

Figure 4.1. Levels of Use of the Innovation

Level 0—Non-use

State in which the individual has little or no knowledge of the innovation, no involvement with it, and is doing nothing toward becoming involved.

DECISION POINT A—Takes action to learn more detailed information about the innovation.
Level I—Orientation

State in which the individual has acquired or is acquiring information about the innovation and/or has explored its value orientation and what it will require.

DECISION POINT B—Makes a decision to use the innovation by establishing a time to begin.
Level II—Preparation

State in which the user is preparing for first use of the innovation.

DECISION POINT C—Begins first use of the innovation.
Level III—Mechanical use

State in which the user focuses most effort on the short-term, day-to-day use of the innovation with little time for reflection. Changes in use are made more to meet user needs than needs of students and others. The user is primarily engaged in an attempt to master tasks required to use the innovation. These attempts often result in disjointed and superficial use.

DECISION POINT D-1—A routine pattern of use is established.
Level IVA—Routine

Use of the innovation is stabilized. Few if any changes are being made in ongoing use. Little preparation or thought is being given to improve innovation use or its consequences.

DECISION POINT D-2—Changes use of the innovation based on format or informal evaluation in order to increase client outcomes.
Level IVB—Refinement

State in which the user varies the use of the innovation to increase the impact on clients (students or others) within their immediate sphere of influence. Variations in use are based on knowledge of both short and long-term consequences for clients.

DECISION POINT E—Initiates changes in use of the innovation based on input from and in coordination with colleagues for benefit of clients.
Level V—Integration

State in which the user is combining own efforts to use the innovation with related activities of colleagues to achieve a collective impact on clients within their common sphere of influence.

DECISION POINT F—Begins exploring alternatives to or major modifications of the innovation presently in use.
Level VI—Renewal

State in which the user reevaluates the quality of use of the innovation, seeks major modifications of, or alternatives to, present innovation to achieve increased impact on clients, examines new developments in the field, and explores new goals for self and the organization.

level encompasses a range of behaviors, but is limited by a decision point that denotes actions that move the individual to the next level. For example, when a person experiences some initiative to learn about an innovation, he or she has reached decision point A and moves from level 0 to level 1.

Assessing Levels of Use

A chart has been developed (Hall, Loucks, Rutherford, and Newlove 1975) that permits the application of a wide variety of information in determining a person's Level of Use. A focused interview is used to acquire the information for the chart. The chart and the focused interview are essential tools for research and quantitative evaluation studies, but such use requires training and certification. People who seek information for the purpose of guiding the implementation of change, on the other hand, can use a combination of observations and informal questioning to get the information needed to determine Levels of Use.

Conversations and Observations

Outcomes from a study of an Intermediate Science Curriculum Study (ISCS) program in a junior high school (Loucks 1977) illustrate how informal observations and questioning can provide information about LoU. In the study a researcher spent an entire day with one teacher collecting information through these informal techniques. Of course, in a typical school setting a facilitator would probably gather this kind of information in "bits and pieces" over time rather than spending an entire day with one teacher. Excerpts from the study notes are presented below. The descriptions in the notes offer two things: they provide a "feel" for the kinds of behaviors persons at each LoU demonstrate, and they illustrate the kinds of information that help determine each level. To better understand the various levels, you may want to refer to the decision points and descriptions for each level in Figure 4.1.

Level of Use 0—Nonuse—Teacher A

The teacher was asked if he used the ISCS science program in any of his classes. He replied, "No," adding that it would have been all right to use a while back, but that redistricting had changed the student population of the school so that the overall student IQ had dropped by ten points. He said that there were kids who would be reading about one page of ISCS every week, "if they could read at all." He then talked about a teacher who had used ISCS in the school four to five years ago. The teacher had left the school, however, and her replacement had just started using ISCS. The replacement, he said, is not convinced that ISCS is the answer, "just like me." When asked if he himself had ever used ISCS in the past, he replied, "No," saying that he was overly traditional. "I've taught science many, many years and have been in the same room almost as many years." He talked about two or three other science innovations that had been tried unsuccessfully in this school. "They were flops," he said. "We spent a lot of money, bought books and equipment, and had to throw it out the window. That's another reason I feel the way I do about ISCS. I have seen too many failures."

Comment: Teacher A seems to know something about ISCS but is making no effort to learn more. In fact, he indicates that he does not plan to use the innovation ever. This absence of any action toward use of the innovation signals clearly LoU 0 (nonuse).

Level of Use I—Orientation—Teacher B

The teacher explained how science was organized in his school and stated that he is considering using ISCS level III. The teacher said he doesn't know the details of ISCS, that he does know about its being self-paced, and that he has visited in ISCS classrooms in a nearby junior high school. Within his building he has also visited classrooms using ISCS levels I and II. While at the other junior high school, he looked at the ninth-grade level III textbooks and was interested in their life science content. He thinks using level III may be a worthwhile thing to do in the future. He has also discussed this briefly with the department chairman at his school, who is currently teaching level II ISCS in the ninth grade. Since Teacher B is interested in life science he is considering ISCS level III. He feels that eighth graders are not mature enough for a self-paced, self-motivating course, and he also remains in favor of having a traditionally taught course between ISCS levels II and III. However, he thinks that ninth graders are more ready for a course like ISCS, and using level III could work at this school.

Comment: Teacher B is definitely taking the initiative to learn more about the innovation and even indicates that he will probably use it sometime in the future. No time has been established for beginning use. If and when he does establish a time to begin use, this teacher will have reached decision point B, which moves him to LoU II. Until that happens he remains at LoU I (orientation).

Level of Use II—Preparation—Teacher C

To begin with, this teacher asked what we expected to learn from a teacher who is not using ISCS materials or programs. She said she's a past user of level I ISCS, but is not now using it at all. She will be teaching two classes of seventh-grade science and three classes of ninth-grade science next year. She will use level I ISCS with the seventh grade and level III ISCS with the ninth grade next year. In a conversation before school, she said she had visited Mr. X's class at another school during the last nine-week period. "He helped me anticipate the problems that might arise in the use of level III ISCS. Also, he helped me order the ninth-grade ISCS materials." She stated that the materials will not arrive until next summer, so Mr. X has loaned her copies of the ISCS level III minibooks. She has looked them over, has started learning more about their content, and will again observe Mr. X teaching in about three weeks. "I feel I can ask his help because I got to know him when I taught his children and, besides, he is doing a lot to help with the ISCS level III program, especially with regard to materials."

Comment: A definite time for beginning use of ISCS has been established, thus decision point B and LoU II (preparation) have been reached. Teacher C is taking steps to get ready to begin use but has not actually started using ISCS. When she actually starts using the program she will have reached decision point C and LoU III.

Level of Use III—Mechanical Use—Teacher D

This teacher said, "I'm just on chapter 8. I know something about chapters 9–12, but some of my students are on chapter 14." She had 5′ × 8′ heavy cardboard cards on a key chain. They were numbered and stopped at chapter 11. She explained she had made the cards because her manual is too awkward to carry around when she is checking student work. These cards have shorthand explanations of each chapter's focus and the answers to specific questions. "We named it the 'Shorthand Key.' " She said she doesn't know the materials well enough to do without it.

In the classroom Teacher D is observed trying to fix test leads for the electrical system. She finds that alligator clips have come off two of them and they are in short supply. Three students are waiting for clips. The teacher goes to her desk and begins to work trying to repair the leads. She takes the leads with her and works on them as she walks about and helps students. A student asks, "What if you use smaller amounts?" And she responds, "Look back in chapter 1. Would it increase? Would it decrease?" Teacher D stops and tells the visiting researcher, "In ISCS you are supposed to ask more questions and give fewer answers, an art I have not perfected." She gets scissors, cuts off the lead wire, and pushes on the alligator clip as she works with a student in the back of the room.

The teacher still works on test leads. Enough leads are temporarily available as some students have finished them.

While the teacher talked, the students asked her a few questions about how to do things, but many about supplies. There was much time spent getting equipment from her desk that only she dispensed. Also, she had to leave the room and go to the supply room three times during this class.

In a few minutes, the teacher arrived carrying a heavy cardboard box. In it she had 21 notebooks. She said the students were going to be disappointed. "They always groan when I don't get their 'end of chapters' graded. I'm always behind."

Comment: Obviously Teacher D is struggling with the management of materials and time as she attempts to use ISCS. She is aware of how the program should work ideally but she is not yet able to use it in that way. This is characteristic of mechanical use of an innovation (LoU III). It is not atypical for teachers to remain at this level for quite some time as they struggle with the logistics of a new program. Once they have mastered the logistics and establish a routine pattern of use they have reached decision point D-1 and have moved to LoU IVA.

Level of Use IVA—Routine—Teacher E

A student brings a test paper to the teacher and they discuss his grade. The teacher suggests he go over the materials once again. He helps him find the correct tote tray. The classroom is well organized. Most of the equipment is labeled to show which ISCS level III book it is for. The ISCS level III books are in a cabinet.

The teacher says that he has the kinks out of the program; he knows what things don't work and has arranged for demonstration or discussion when kids get to them.

He also says he has not made any changes in what he is doing, that since the first year, using ISCS has been pretty much the same. He says that there are some things he could refine; for example, his tests need some minor changes, but he feels that since the better kids do well on them, they must be all right. He says he really doesn't need plans since everything is organized and ready to use and the students all know where they are in the program.

Comment: This teacher has reached routine use (LoU IVA) of ISCS and intends to make no changes. He states that his tests might be refined a bit but he does not really plan to do that. Once a user reaches the routine Level of Use it is not uncommon to remain there for an extended time, making only minor adjustments in patterns of use. Other users, after reaching this level, will begin to vary their use of the innovation in an effort to improve outcomes. Users who make these kinds of changes have reached decision point D-2 and are now at LoU IVB.

Level of Use IVB—Refinement—Teacher F

Teacher F spent half of the period walking around, helping when needed. The kids appeared to be working on different chapters in their books. Some were reading and writing; most had set up equipment and were working. They worked individually and only one or two pairs were observed. All were constructively involved.

The teacher appeared to get around to many kids each period, but also spent as much time with each one as seemed necessary. The teacher aide said things were very well organized. Teacher F rarely had to do anything with equipment, since it's all set.

The teacher told me she had been teaching two years and had had no formal training in ISCS. She said she'd still like a minicourse in the next ISCS level (level III) where she could go through each experiment like a kid. She said she thought that would give her a better perspective on what her kids would learn in later years. She also plans to visit some high school classrooms to find out what the kids do in high school so she can help hers be better prepared.

The teacher described a change she had made in the last couple of months. She had decided that the kids would learn more and be more independent if they didn't work in pairs. She therefore had them work individually, and if they needed help with the equipment only, they could help each other. She said that even if this made some accomplish less than before, they still would do their own work and feel success in their own right.

She plans to create some extra units for next year so that the kids will have a break from the individual pacing and will be able to learn some of the other aspects of science that ISCS leaves out. She mentioned that the kids expressed an interest in animals and weather—two units she would like to try to do.

Comment: Having the students work individually rather than in pairs was a variation in use of the innovation Teacher F made because she believed it would benefit the students. Because the change in use was for the benefit of the clients (students), Teacher F is said to be at LoU IVB (refinement). Had she made changes to solve some management problems or to make her own teaching day less hectic she would not be at LoU IVB but at LoU III (mechanical use).

Level of Use V—Integration—Teacher G

Teacher G, who was being observed, and her team teacher, Mr. X, are teaming for the first time this year. As students come into the room, Mr. X is in the west end of the room discussing supplies with the girl in charge of checking materials out of the storeroom. Teacher G is near the door greeting students as they come in. They stop to talk with her and each other. A few get workbooks, go to the seating section in the east end, and begin to work. Mr. X goes to the front of the room. He quickly determines who is absent. He asks students to do a better job of cleaning up tables at the end of the hour and putting away all textbooks. He asks Teacher G if she has any announcements. She shakes her head.

Teacher G sits at a desk and Mr. X looks over her shoulder as she shows him David's workbook. David has left it with her on his way to the storeroom. Mr. X: "It is amazing." Teacher G: "I don't know." Both leave the desk to respond to two separate groups of students.

A small fire breaks out at one table. Both teachers are there instantly. Mr. X stands back and asks George, "What are you doing about it?" George is frozen. Mr. X takes the fire extinguisher and puts the fire out. Teacher G was so near that she got residue from the chemicals on her clothes. Mr. X reviews fire rules with the class.

Teacher G said that recently several students had told her that Mr. X was an easier grader then she. She felt that would not be good for the students, so she and he checked and informally evaluated their grading. They found it comparable, but want to be sure they expect the same standards for ISCS in order to have a unified effect on students.

Teacher G has the feeling that she is experiencing a growing capacity to make a difference in the lives of her students. She thinks ISCS and teaming provide the best possible vehicle for doing that.

Comment: These teachers decided on their own to collaborate because they thought that by so doing they could provide better learning experiences for their students. LoU V (integration) is determined by two key variables: collaboration between two or more persons and changes in use of the innovation for the benefit of clients. Furthermore, the collaboration must be regular, not just a casual conversation every couple of weeks. Because most teachers tend to work as "solitary craftsmen," the number of persons at LoU V is typically small.

Level of Use VI—Renewal—Teacher H

After a bell rang, signaling the beginning of the first period, the teacher and the visiting researcher walked down the hall from the teachers' lounge to his classroom. There, they began to talk about ISCS as he prepared his classroom for the day. He said that he had taught at the junior high school for eight years and that this was his fourth year using ISCS. When asked how he liked the program, he replied, "Oh, not really. I don't dislike it, but then I'm really not sure of what I think would be better. I have an idea."

He then went to the chalkboard and began to describe a model for teaching ninth-grade physical science. He described his model as a combination of traditional elements and ISCS. At the beginning of each unit of study, students would be together for an introduction by the teacher through a traditional lecture/demonstration format. They would then be presented with a number of labs of varying degrees of difficulty from which they would be able to choose one that would suit their learning style and abilities. They would be allowed to work either independently or with other students. Labs would be self-paced. Once the lab work was completed, the students would be pulled together again for a summary discussion by the teacher, a general class discussion of their lab work, and perhaps oral reports by individual students. The whole unit would take between three and five weeks. The teacher felt that this plan would allow for a type of student interaction lacking in ISCS. It would also give him a chance to work with the class as a whole.

"Maybe one could borrow some ISCS ideas and use them in combination with the traditional as a synthesis of the old and the new." He then discussed a new program that is scheduled to begin the next school year. "We are talking about starting an accelerated science class next year, possibly at each level (seventh, eighth, and ninth). I think this is good and I think that we are slowly realizing that the good students have something coming too. We need to have programs for them as well as for the poor students."

Comment: Clearly Teacher H has some ideas for major changes in his use of ISCS. The reasons for the changes are focused on students and what he feels they need to improve learning. It is important to note that although he is thinking about, talking about, and planning these changes, they have not actually occurred. In this regard LoU VI (renewal) is different from LoU IVB (refinement). Once this teacher actually makes the proposed changes, he will probably be dealing with another innovation, not ISCS, and his Level of Use will recycle based on that innovation.

Using an Informal Interview

For those facilitators who may not have the opportunity to gather the kinds of information presented in the above vignettes, the informal LoU interview (Figure 4.2) can be a useful tool. This interview frame-

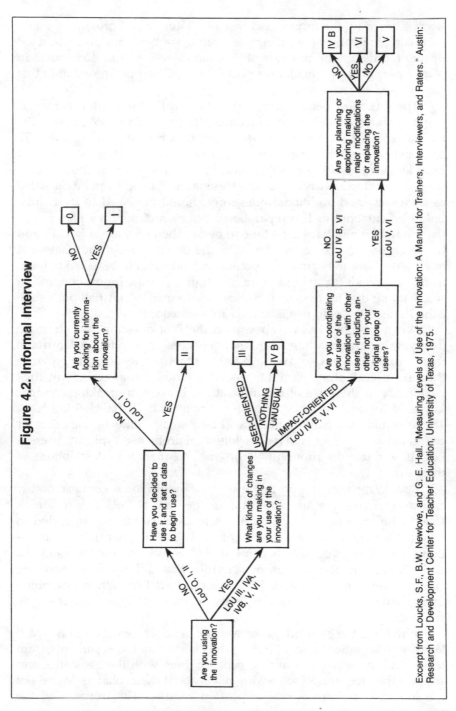

Figure 4.2. Informal Interview

Excerpt from Loucks, S.F., B.W. Newlove, and G. E. Hall. "Measuring Levels of Use of the Innovation: A Manual for Trainers, Interviewers, and Raters." Austin: Research and Development Center for Teacher Education, University of Texas, 1975.

work is based on the formal LoU research interview. It provides a guide for talking to people about their use of an innovation, and it can be used by any facilitator. The purpose of such an interview is to do more than place a person at a particular Level of Use; it will supply information that can be used to facilitate use.

The interview begins with a question to find out if the person is using the innovation. (Beyond just accepting a "yes" or "no" answer, the facilitator might ask for a brief description of how it is being used. To accurately assess the response to this question, the facilitator should have knowledge of the configuration of the innovation as described in chapter 2). If the answer to this question is "no," people can be classified as nonusers, and additional questions should be asked to determine LoU I (orientation) or II (preparation). If they indicate they plan to use the innovation and have set a time to begin, then they are at LoU II, and the interview can be terminated. On the other hand, if they have not made a decision to begin use, another question should be asked to learn if they are seeking any kind of information about the innovation and, if so, what kind. The person who seeks information but has not estab- lished a time to begin use is at LoU I (orientation).

When people say in response to the first question that they are using the innovation, then additional questions are needed to determine their actual Level of Use. We have found that the question that provides the most useful information it to ask what kinds of changes, if any, they have made in their use of the innovation. If users are making changes intended for their own benefit, they are at LoU III (mechanical use). These would be changes in how they manage time or materials or classroom arrangements to reduce logistical problems. Typically, users at LoU III will use the pronoun "I" or "me" frequently in descriptions of their use.

Should the users report that use of the innovation is going smoothly and no real changes are being made, they are at LoU IVA (routine). Users who respond with descriptions of changes that are intended to help the learner in some way are at LoU IVB (refinement). Reorganiza- tion of a unit, resequencing of content, addition of enrichment materials, and elimination of materials or activities that did not work well are changes commonly mentioned by users at LoU IVB. When describing their changes, these users are likely to make frequent reference to students.

Although the percentage of innovation users who actually reach levels V (integration) and VI (renewal) is fairly small, it is still important to identify those persons and to provide them with the assistance and support they require. When asking users about their collaborative use of the innovation, there is one important caution. The purpose of the integration or collaboration must be for the benefit of students if the individual is to be classified at LoU V. Often two or more users will work together to solve their management problems. Those who collaborate to serve their own needs are at LoU III (mechanical), not LoU V. Also, the collaboration must be regular and ongoing. Meeting together and sharing once a month or whenever it is convenient do not represent LoU V behaviors.

If users are not at Lou V, continue with your questioning, for they could be at LoU VI (renewal). Those individuals who are at LoU VI will often flood you with ideas and information about the changes they have in mind. The ideas they have are often for a change to a different program. At the least, they will call for significant modifications in the existing innovation. You will frequently hear them say the changes will be better or work better for students. These people are exciting to talk to.

In Springdale, the informal LoU interview was used in May to assess how teachers were progressing with their use of the effective teaching program. The outcomes of these interviews are summarized as follows:

LoU 0	LoU I	LoU II	LoU III	LoU IVA	LoU IVB	LoU V	LoU VI
5%	0	5%	65%	20%	5%	0	0

These data have important implications for the facilitators of the effective teaching program as discussed below.

Levels of Use and the Facilitation of Change

The Level of Use dimension of the CBAM offers information that can be of great assistance to any change facilitator. Levels of Use are a reality; they exist for each individual in relation to each innovation. Even if ignored, they persist; they do not disappear. When ignored, however, Levels of Use will take their own course, one that may well be counterproductive to the implementation effort and to the intended outcomes of an innovation. Therefore, it behooves all change facilitators to give serious consideration to Levels of Use.

Of course, many factors may influence a person's and group's Levels of Use, but the most powerful influence is the manner in which the implementation is facilitated. Before discussing some specific ways in which Levels of Use might be facilitated, some general knowledge about use and change should be considered.

People tend to move sequentially (if they move at all) from LoU 0 (nonuse) to LoU IVA (routine). From that point, they may move to a higher level or they may move "back" to a lower level. There is a greater probability, however, that they will remain at that level. After an innovation has been in use for some time, we find that the majority of users (excluding nonusers) in a sample at any one time will be at LoU IVA (routine). But change does not occur easily or quickly. As a general rule, 60 to 70 percent of the first-year users of an innovation will be at the mechanical level (LoU III). This is reflected in the Springdale data presented above. When the innovation is reasonably complex, as is the Springdale effective teaching program, many users are likely to continue at LoU III beyond the first year.

Unless the innovation itself calls for collaboration among users (such as in team teaching), usually few users will reach LoU V (integration). Even fewer users reach LoU VI (renewal), and those who do may not remain there long. When they act on their ideas they usually create a new innovation for themselves, and their Level of Use will recycle based on that innovation.

A final and important warning for change facilitators: do not assume people will use an innovation just because it has been introduced. Research conducted in hundreds of schools and involving many innovations has revealed that it is quite common to find at least 20 percent of the teachers in any school who are nonusers even in the second and third years of implementation. Often the percentage of nonusers is much higher.

A good starting point for change facilitators is with nonusers. The facilitator must first decide if he or she wants and expects these teachers to use the innovation. Assuming this is answered in the affirmative, interventions should be directed at moving the nonusers to user levels. At LoU 0, intended users should be made aware of the impending innovation and the expectation that it be used by all. Ideally, potential users will be involved in developing or at least deciding on the innovation, but this is not often the case with innovations mandated from district- or state-level officials. Individuals at the school level often learn about the innovation from an announcement by the in-school facilitator.

At the orientation and preparation levels (LoU I and II), people need information at two levels. First, they need to be aware of the innovation as a whole, its general requirements and purposes, and the timelines for its implementation. At this level it is important not to overwhelm people with too much information. Make it look possible, not impossible, to implement. Also, do not dwell on how effective the innovation has been somewhere else. This only puts unnecessary pressures on the potential users by implying that if they don't use it successfully right away, they are failures.

Next, after receiving general information about the innovation, and as they move closer to initial use, people need specific information about the basic steps for using the innovation and any materials or equipment that will be required. Also, it would be good to give them some idea of what the innovation will look like when in use. Keep the focus on immediate use, not ultimate, perfected use, and direct your assistance to their classroom, not to some generalized or theoretical situation.

As first use begins and for some time thereafter, the user is likely to be at the mechanical level (LoU III). Precisely what kind of assistance will be needed at this level will depend to a great extent on the innovation and its requirements. In any event the users will probably be staying just one step ahead of the students in terms of planning and preparations. This may be because they are attempting to use new materials or trying a new plan for classroom organization that makes the management of time and students difficult. It can be beneficial for users at this level to observe other teachers who have worked out similar problems or at least to receive their verbal guidance. Workshops that focus on such problems can also be helpful. Bringing together small groups of teachers with common problems with a facilitator can provide needed technical assistance as well as build a mutual support system. Comfort and caring is one way to describe the kind of assistance needed at LoU III (mechanical use).

People who are at routine use (LoU IVA) typically do not seek assistance, for their use of the innovation is going along rather smoothly. Even so, they should not be forgotten or ignored. If their use is satisfactory and meets the expectations of the facilitator, the user should at least receive the recognition and praise of the facilitator for her or his performance. Check with these users to see if there is anything that can be provided for them that would make their use of the innovation easier or better. Perhaps they would like to have more materials of some sort or would like advice about some of the things they are doing. Even if they accept no assistance, these users will appreciate the attention and concern and that, in turn, will reinforce the fact that using the innovation is important.

A word of caution about users at LoU IVA. It is not uncommon that some of these users will move rather quickly to this level by implementing a less than ideal configuration of the innovation and then stabilizing their performance at that level. For these users, the facilitator should not be too generous with praise and recognition, but should encourage more effective use of the innovation. For example, in Springdale's effective teaching program, some teachers may have established a step-by-step procedure for teaching content with which they are comfortable, but their pacing of the steps may be such that it does not accommodate student differences. A facilitator should intervene to help the teachers improve their pacing. Be aware that because these LoU IVA users are not likely to be particularly interested in modifying their use, they may have to be encouraged to change at the same time they are being assisted in doing so.

LoU IVB (refinement) users are fun to work with, for they usually are excited about their use of the innovation. They are making shifts and moderate changes in their use, which they like to talk about. From the facilitator these users need sanction and support for their improvement efforts along with positive reinforcement. One way to support and reinforce is to arrange for these users to visit in other schools or classrooms where they might get new ideas or models for what they are trying to do. Allow others to visit in their classroom, for they will be good models for other users. They can also be effective in helping users who may be having difficulty with the innovation.

Levels of Use V (integration) and VI (renewal) require special consideration from the facilitator, for they are different in some key ways. Because these users differ from the previous six levels, facilitators are cautioned not to move too quickly or vigorously to promote these levels. Movement to these levels is not always desirable or possible.

LoU V (integration) cannot be reached by one user alone. There must be one or more others with whom the user is collaborating. Often collaborative use of an innovation stems from previous sharing relationships between the parties. At other times, the collaboration develops spontaneously as a result of common needs or interests. When LoU V occurs in these ways, the role of the facilitator is one of supporting the arrangement. One way this can be done is by arranging for the time the users might need for joint planning and decision making. If the collaboration involves shared teaching times or shared students, the facilitator can assist by making modifications in the daily schedule. Should the collaboration involve a group, the users may well benefit from workshops or materials that offer guidelines for managing groups.

When collaborative arrangements are desired or expected but do not occur naturally or spontaneously, the role of the facilitator will change somewhat. Instead of being in a supporting role, the facilitator will have to become a promoter of collaboration. But before this is done, the facilitator should consider whether collaboration is essential to effective use of the innovation. Planned cooperation between users can be rewarding apart from any particular innovation, but formal, planned efforts to promote collaboration in connection with an innovation can be counterproductive. Collaboration, if overly stressed, may become an innovation in itself, and the user is put in the position of having to implement two innovations. This does not mean that a facilitator should not promote collaboration, only that it should be done carefully and with an awareness of purpose. Having users share with others the advantages and rewards of collaboration is one way to promote interest. If others show an interest, the facilitator can provide more details about the ways they can share and what steps they might take to accomplish the process.

For several reasons, facilitators are not likely to devote much time to encouraging users to the renewal level (LoU VI). First, the limited number of people who reach this level usually do so as a result of their own initiative and creativity. Second, users at LoU VI are seeking to replace the innovation or significantly modify it, and this could be disruptive to the efforts of the facilitator who is attempting to help users attain maximum effective use of the innovation. It must be strongly emphasized that in the majority of cases, LoU VI users are a positive force, not a negative force, in the implementation effort. This is especially true if they are viewed positively and not as a threat.

Facilitators who take time to interact with users at this level will be well rewarded. These people not only have creative ideas, but ideas that are usually also logical and sound. Most of all, these users have a sincere concern for their students, and they are dedicated to enhancing their learning opportunities. Their excitement is uplifting and some of their ideas can be beneficial to other users. LoU VI users can be helped by putting them into contact with other users at this level or with other persons who have knowledge that will enrich their thinking. Make available to them any new materials they may be interested in using, or sponsor their attendance at workshops where they can gain information related to their plans. Helping them channel their ideas and energies in a logical and productive manner will also be valuable.

Levels of Use and Implementation Monitoring

The suggestions above are provided for those who facilitate the change efforts of individuals and groups. Another important use for the Levels of Use dimension of CBAM is assessing innovation implementation. If this is to be done in a rigorous manner, the evaluators should have formal LoU training.

The information thus derived about the Levels of Use of all persons in a school or a district can then be used to guide the interpretation of innovation outcomes. If a significant percentage of users have not reached routine use (IVA or above), it might be advisable to delay outcome evaluations or at least to interpret such evaluations in light of the distribution of Levels of Use. For example, if many of the users are at LoU III (mechanical use), it means they are still struggling with the "nuts and bolts" of innovation use. Under those circumstances it is not likely the innovation will have a positive influence on students and produce high student outcomes. As shown in the Springdale data collected in May, 75 percent of the teachers were at LoU III or below, making it improbable that the effective teaching program would at that time reflect a positive difference in student outcomes.

Levels of Use data can reveal problems that may exist in the implementation process. In our own research we found schools where fewer than 50 percent of the teachers were actually using an innovation, even in the second year. In other schools a high percentage of users were not moving beyond the mechanical level (LoU III). Still other data revealed some obvious differences in the Levels of Use distribution for the same innovation, but in different schools. In each of these cases, the differences in use seemed to be attributable, at least in part, to the manner in which the innovation was facilitated.

Whether it be for facilitating the performance of individual users or for evaluating implementation, the Levels of Use dimension of CBAM is a unique tool that can be valuable to any facilitator responsible for implementing an innovation.

Questions Often Asked about Levels of Use

Q: *Can you really determine Levels of Use through an interview? Will people honestly describe what they are doing?*

A: Our experience has been that they are more than willing to talk with someone about their use of an innovation and what they are doing with it. However, they may not share with you the kind of information you seek unless you ask for it. This is why the suggested interview questions are so useful. People do not intentionally withhold information as a rule, but they may not be thinking along the same lines as you are.

Q: *Is there a questionnaire that can be used to assess Levels of Use?*

A: No, there is not. Several attempts have been made to develop a questionnaire that would accurately assess LoU, but none has succeeded. This is because the phenomenon does not match paper-and-pencil measurement. It is similar to trying to read semaphore signals by turning on a radio. The personal interview, coupled with observations when possible, offers the most accurate and useful information.

Q: *Can users ever go from a "higher" Level of Use to a "lower" one?*

A: Yes, they certainly can. People who are at the orientation level (LoU I) may decide not to use the innovation, at which time they move to nonuse (LoU 0). Persons who have real problems using the innovation and cannot seem to move beyond the mechanical level (LoU III) likely will become weary or frustrated and become nonusers. People who have made recent changes that place them at the refinement level (LoU IVB) will automatically return to LoU IVA (routine) once those changes have stabilized and they are making no other changes. When people at LoU VI (renewal) actually make the changes they have planned, they are no longer at LoU VI but will recycle to a "lower" level with their new program. Persons can abandon use of the innovation from any level for a number of reasons. Other shifts in LoU are possible, but these are the most likely.

5.
The Role of Effective Change Facilitators

In preparing her end-of-the-year report to the school board, Assistant Superintendent Jenkins organized and analyzed the data that had been collected. She felt satisfied that good progress had been made, despite the fact that she had had to "play it by ear" much of the time. For year two, though, she wanted to be more systematic in order to make the most of her limited resources and increase the probabilities for long-term success.

Moreover, she was concerned about the board. To win their continuing support, and to help them understand the complexities of the change process, she needed to present more than her first-year data. She needed a plan for the coming year, one that was clear, comprehensive, and grounded in the outcomes of this year's efforts. She decided to investigate another CBAM tool, the Intervention Taxonomy, that could help her outline both long-term strategies and day-to-day activities needed to support implementation.

DRIVEN BY COMMITMENT, ENERGY, AND AN INNATE SENSE OF WHAT might work, Springdale's assistant superintendent for instruction provided strong leadership, appropriate facilitation, and useful management in overseeing implementation of the new program. Many of Jenkins's activities, however, stemmed from trial and error and what she intuitively thought was "right." Although she was able to find and use the CBAM diagnostic tools (SoC, LoU, IC) and to accomplish a great deal, she could have saved time, resources, and frustration if she had begun her task with a comprehensive *game plan*.

One of the major contentions of this book is that guesswork and intuition need not be the CF's only touchstones. We now know a great deal about how to plan for and manage change more efficiently and effectively. As the previous chapters illustrate, there are techniques and tools that can support your role as facilitator, helping you provide appropriate assistance to those who are implementing change. You may use these approaches either singly or in combination in many different circumstances. Ideally, though, you would integrate these concepts and tools into an overall scheme, or game plan, that provides you, the CF, with a blueprint for action.

Your game plan would outline all the kinds of interventions necessary to facilitate change. It would list both long-term and short-term strategies. Finally, it would identify a team of facilitators and designate responsibilities for each team member. No plan, of course, can predict or control everything that might happen, but with what is now known about change, you can do much to anticipate and prepare for the process.

The earlier chapters of this book focused on ways in which you, the CF, can help teachers do their jobs in effectively implementing change. This chapter is intended to help you do your job. It offers ideas and tools for considering the dimensions of the facilitator's role. It suggests who within your district or school might be likely to function as a facilitator, and in what capacities. It provides tools and formats for planning what to do and when. Together with the other CBAM approaches described in this book, the materials in this chapter offer you a basic framework for facilitating school improvement. Like the rest of the book, these materials are based on our research in actual school settings.

What Facilitators of Change Do

We spent several years in a number of schools, documenting the actions (interventions) associated with implementing curriculum programs, behavior processes, and other innovations. From these studies, we identified six distinct categories of interventions. We call these categories game plan components (GPC), because collectively they account for a total change effort (Hall and Hord 1984). Each category contains many different actions that can be taken by change facilitators; collectively, they describe what CFs do. (See Figure 5.1 for a quick sketch of the

Figure 5.1. A Checklist of Suggested CF Actions to Support Change

GPC 1: Developing Supportive Organizational Arrangements

developing innovation-related policies
establishing global rules
making decisions
planning
preparing
scheduling
staffing
restructuring roles
seeking or providing materials
providing space
seeking/acquiring funds
providing equipment

GPC 2: Training

developing positive attitudes
increasing knowledge
teaching innovation-related skills
reviewing information
holding workshops
modeling/demonstrating innovation use
observing innovation use
providing feedback on innovation use
clarifying innovation misconceptions

GPC 3: Consultation and Reinforcement

encouraging people on a one-to-one basis
promoting innovation use among small groups
assisting individuals in solving problems
coaching small groups in innovation use
sharing tips informally
providing personalized technical assistance
holding brief conversations and applauding
    progress
facilitating small groups in problem solving
providing small "comfort and caring" sessions
reinforcing individuals' attempts to change
providing practical assistance
celebrating small successes (or large ones, too)

GPC 4: Monitoring

gathering information
collecting data
assessing innovation knowledge or skills
    informally
assessing innovation use or concerns formally
analyzing/processing data
interpreting information
reporting/sharing data on outcomes
providing feedback on information collected
administering end-of-workshop questionnaires
conferencing with teachers about progress in
    innovation use

GPC 5: External Communication

describing what the innovation is
informing others (than users)
reporting to the Board of Education and parent
    groups
making presentations at conferences
developing a public relations campaign
gaining the support of constituent groups

GPC 6: Dissemination

encouraging others (outside the implementing
    site) to adopt the innovation
broadcasting innovation information and
    materials
mailing descriptive brochures
providing charge-free demonstration kits
training innovation representatives
making regional innovation presentations to
    potential adopters
marketing the innovation

types of intervention activities found in each GPC.) Each game plan component is explained in more detail in the following pages.

GPC 1: Developing Supportive Organizational Arrangements

The interventions in this component will be quite familiar to those of you who facilitate teachers' work. They include providing for space, materials, personnel, equipment or furniture—all the things needed before implementation can begin. They also include ongoing actions to supply materials and maintain arrangements after implementation is under way. Developing guidelines, regulations, and policies related to the innovation, acquiring funding and other unique resources, planning for the change, and managing the process are all essential parts of this component. As our case study suggests, acquiring the resources necessary to support new programs often turns out to be the greatest challenge in this GPC. The Springdale School Board provided barely half the funding Jenkins requested and expected the program to be on its feet within a single year. Because most programs need resources on an ongoing basis, you may find yourself developing skills in the "creative" acquisition of resources. For instance, one facilitator we observed engaged parent volunteers to assist in organizing and preparing materials for teachers. Another facilitator "broadly interpreted" the guidelines for dispersal of funds in order to provide much needed equipment to teachers.

GPC 2: Training

No matter how abundant and appealing materials may be, with most innovations teachers need training to understand clearly how to use them. Moreover, training should be an ongoing process to enable teachers to grow and to continue developing new skills. To be most effective, training designs must take into account teachers' individual needs and concerns. A single, generalized training session prior to a new program's initial use is rarely adequate to ensure effective implementation, no matter how "comprehensive" or "in depth" it is advertised to be.

Included in the training GPC are the structured, preplanned activities, such as workshops and demonstration sessions, designed to develop innovation-related knowledge, performance skills, and positive attitudes. Effective CFs arrange for training for all involved persons: teachers, adminstrators, supervisors, coordinators, and others who have a role in the change.

GPC 3: Consultation and Reinforcement

Consultation and reinforcement are less formal, more specific, and more personalized than training. These intervention activities are one-to-one, or aimed at very small groups, and frequently are provided as a follow-up to training. They are designed to address the unique needs of individual teachers. Some CFs have called these activities "comfort and caring," or "at-the-elbow assistance."

Consultation sessions should fill the gaps between training opportunities, and continue until the novice develops into an experienced, effective user of an innovation. Consultation may consist of brief, informal conversations with teachers about "how it's going"; the facilitator may share tips, provide practical assistance, or compliment and reinforce the teacher's progress. This informal, personalized support and attention can be critical to successful implementation.

GPC 4: Monitoring

The effective CFs we observed in our studies sought objective data to help them assess progress in implementing their new programs. They gathered information about what was happening with an innovation and about the status and progress of teachers as they were introduced to, started working with, and became experienced in using new school practices. Though the importance of monitoring activities is gaining increased recognition, particularly through recent research on effective principals (Rutherford 1985), this category of intervention is often neglected. Some principals hesitate to monitor their staffs, declaring, "My teachers are professionals; I leave them alone." Interestingly, these teachers often report feeling ignored and abandoned by their principals. Monitoring does not have to be a threat to teachers; it can be an informal process, carried out by the principal or by other facilitators. But monitoring must take place to ensure a successful improvement effort.

What can you do to monitor? In chapters 3 and 4 we discussed one-legged conferences with teachers (described in chapter 3 as one-to-one or face-to-face conversations, and in chapter 4 as the informal LoU interview). These can be used to assess concerns and Levels of Use, and to find out what configurations of an innovation are in operation. The configuration component checklist is an excellent monitoring tool to determine which program components and their variations teachers are using. The open-ended concerns statement technique provides written data about teachers' concerns and valuable information about their progress. You can also monitor the effects of training interventions by eliciting end-of-workshop reactions, or using a follow-up survey after an inservice session.

After teachers start to use a new program or practice, monitoring activity can be influential in reminding teachers that their attention is required for the program. It helps teachers recognize that the improvement project is a priority, that a commitment has been made to it, and that somebody cares about them, about the change, and how it is occurring in classrooms. Monitoring is also a natural complement to consultation/reinforcement in that it provides valuable data about how individuals are doing and what their assistance needs might be.

The four GPCs, or intervention categories, discussed above are those we found in our observations to be vital to successful change. They are important elements in any effort to implement innovations, and therefore demand the attention of every CF. The following two game plan components are important to many, but not necessarily all, school improvement efforts. The extent to which you as a CF need to focus on these two GPCs will depend on the nature of the innovation and on your school, district, or community environment.

GPC 5: External Communication

These interventions are made to inform or gain the support of individuals or groups external to the school where the innovation is being implemented. The activities focus on describing the school improvement project, plans for its management, and its potential impact. These actions may include developing a public relations campaign, reporting to a parent group or board of education, or making presentations at conferences. The usual goal of interventions in this GPC is to maintain the support of various constituencies.

GPC 6: Dissemination

Some schools take actions to "broadcast" information about the school improvement program or practice in order to encourage others to adopt the new practice. These efforts may involve mailing descriptive brochures to potential adoptees, offering demonstration materials, or even training and providing regional innovation representatives to support others in adopting and implementing innovations.

Frequently when a school develops a new program, puts it into use, and verifies its effectiveness, a decision is made to submit it to outside reviewers, such as the Federal Joint Dissemination Review Panel (JDRP). If the program is approved by the JDRP, then federal funds are provided to support dissemination activities and adoption of the program by others via the National Diffusion Network (NDN). Many successful teacher-developed programs are transplanted to other school sites through the NDN strategy.

Other Models for Describing What Change Facilitators Do

To check our perceptions and views of the schools, and to make sure we had described all the kinds of interventions needed for successful change, we reviewed the literature to identify other actions that change facilitators might carry out. This review revealed some interesting information. Gersten and Carnine (1981), for example, concluded that particular "support" functions are needed if the change process is to be successful:

. . . one can derive from the existing literature a listing of those behaviors and policies of administrators and supervisors that appear to be necessary for innovations to be implemented and sustained (p. 21).

Figure 5.2. A Comparison of Identified Functions for Effective Leadership

Gersten and Carnine (1981) Support Functions	Gall et al. (1984) Instructional Leadership Functions	Hall and Hord (1984) Intervention Game Plan Components
Visible commitment	Priority setting	
Incentive systems	Resource acquisition	Developing supportive organizational arrangements
	Institutional policy-making	
	Training	Training
Technical assistance		Consultation and reinforcement
Monitoring	Monitoring	Monitoring and evaluation
	Assessment	
	External relations	External communication
		Dissemination
Explicit strategies		
	Compliance	
	Maintenance	

Adapted from Hall and Hord 1986

They identified five categories of these behaviors. Similarly, Gall and colleagues (1984) identified a set of "leadership" functions they found to be associated with implementation and effective staff development programs. As Figure 5.2 demonstrates, there is a great deal of similarity between the findings of other researchers and the CBAM game plan components. These results reflect a growing consensus about actions required to support the change process.

Game Planning with the Components

In identifying the categories of interventions that CFs carry out, we have used the phrase *game plan components* with purpose. Our expectation is that you, as a change facilitator, not only will be involved in providing services to support change; you also will be actively engaged in planning for the change. Your role will be not unlike that of an athletic coach who prepares a game plan (often with input from assistant coaches and sometimes from the players themselves) and then offers advice and assistance in carrying it out.

We are recommending the game plan components as a practical, easy-to-use framework to guide school improvement planning, with particular attention to components 1–4 (Hord and Huling-Austin 1986). There is more to planning for change, however, than making certain that interventions from the different game plan components are designed and delivered. It is important to consider both the long-term and short-range dimensions of planning.

Long-term or strategic plans. Strategies may be thought of as representing objectives to be accomplished in the change process. Strategies are expressed in terms of concrete outcomes to be attained over a substantial period of time (one school year of more); they address most or all of the individuals involved in a particular change process. An effective and comprehensive game plan includes strategy statements for each game plan component. For example, under the training GPC, strategies/objectives might be (1) during year one, administrators will receive training in managing the school improvement project; and (2) teachers will receive periodic hands-on training throughout year one in how to use effective teaching steps 1, 3, and 4.

Short-range or incident plans. Incidents are what might typically be called "enabling activities"; that is, they are the specific interventions that make it possible to accomplish the larger strategy. They are of much shorter duration than strategies; they may affect one, or few, or many persons. Many incidents can be planned for at the beginning of a change effort; others are planned during ongoing planning/review sessions; and some are designed on the spur of the moment as the need or opportunity arises.

Effective CFs look for and recognize opportunities to provide incident interventions. For example, when you meet a teacher unexpectedly in the parking lot, take a moment to ask, "Has last week's training helped you? Can I provide some assistance?" Too often, facilitators neglect to recognize the frequent opportunities available to make these modest, but powerfully important interventions. A single incident may not carry a great amount of weight, but collectively they add up and can be extremely influential. And they should add up—as you are developing your plans, focus on incidents that, across time, have some continuity and that geometrically increase in impact.

You will find that both long-range strategic plans and short-range incident plans are important to the success of your change efforts and that the two must complement each other to be truly effective. We have observed planning at the strategy/objectives level that never influenced the change process because no incident plans were developed to put it into operation. At the other extreme, we have seen CFs plan and deliver a multiplicity of incidents, all types in all directions, without a larger focus to guide them. We have also seen change projects that had neither long-term nor short-range planning; chance reigned, frequently ruining a promising school improvement effort.

With the individual and innovation in mind. As you begin developing strategies and incidents for each game plan component, consider also your concerns-based diagnostic information—SoC, LoU, IC. As suggested in earlier chapters, we can predict how teachers' concerns and use generally evolve over the course of a school improvement project; this knowledge can help you as you construct your initial intervention game plan. Because not all individuals follow the typical patterns, however, you will need to use the SoC, LoU, and IC tools periodically to assess each person and redesign your interventions as needed.

Using the IC checklist that has been developed to describe and define the components of an innovation (see chapter 2) can also help you make decisions about your intervention game plan. For example, the components to be implemented next month will require immediate ordering of material, while other materials can wait. Similarly, you will need to schedule training for the innovation components to be implemented first, while training related to components that are not "on-line" for implementation can be held for later attention. In addition to using the checklist to make decisions about which innovation components to attend to first and at what speed, you can also use it to monitor the status of the new practice in each classroom and to adjust the game plan as necessary.

A skeleton of a game plan that you may find helpful as you develop your own plans is included in Figure 5.3. First, consider and develop strategies for each game plan component. Write your strategies in the space suggested (an enlarged edition of this skeleton would be more useful than the small page we have provided). Then think of incidents to activate the strategy—incidents that take into account the SoC/LoU/IC diagnoses of teachers. It is not necessary to make an exhaustive list of incidents. Many of these will be designed as you do your short-term, day-to-day planning; others will emerge as the moment presents itself. The importance of the game plan at this point is to develop long-range strategies that will provide a framework for your actions as facilitator, and to identify a few key incidents to put your strategies into operation. The incidents, by and large, will come later, shaped to individuals' SoC, LoU and IC.

Figure 5.3. Skeleton of a Concerns-Based Game Plan

	SoC 0,1,2 LoU 0,I,II IC	SoC 3 LoU III IC	SoC Flat LoU IVA IC	SoC 4,5,6 Lou IVB,V,VI IC
Game Plan Component 1: Strategy(s) Developing Supportive Organizational Arrangements	Incident(s) Incident(s) Incident(s)	Incident(s) Incident(s) Incident(s)	Incident(s) Incident(s) Incident(s)	Incident(s) Incident(s) Incident(s)
Game Plan Component 2: Strategy(s) Training	" " "	" " "	" " "	" " "

	Strategy(s)			
Game Plan Component 3: Providing Consultation and Reinforcement				
Game Plan Component 4: Monitoring and Evaluation				
Game Plan Component 5: External Communication				
Game Plan Component 6: Dissemination				

Adapted from: Hord and Loucks 1980.

The Facilitator Team: Who Can Act to Facilitate Change

Much attention has been devoted to the importance of the principal's role in the process of school improvement. In our studies, we extensively observed principals in the role of change facilitator. We found effective principals constantly surveying their domain and gathering information about the setting, the staff, and the students. They processed what they saw and generated ideas about how to address problems and needs that they had observed. Furthermore, effective principals shared responsibilities and leadership with others on their staff. Effective principals are collaborators; they are also delegators, carefully and thoughtfully identifying and utilizing available human resources.

In our early studies we thought principals were the only "key to change" in the school. To our surprise, we found others—school- and central office-based staff and administrators—playing significant roles in support of teacher change. These persons we labeled the *second change facilitators*, or second CF (Hord, Stiegelbauer, and Hall 1984). (Because of their position, power, and influence, we identified principals as the first CF.) The second CF was sometimes the assistant principal, sometimes department or grade-level chairs, resource teachers, or teachers on special assignment. At the district level, second CFs were often curriculum or subject coordinators or supervisors, or specially named innovation facilitators. Whether this second CF (second "in command") position was filled by a school-based or district-based person usually related to the amount of activity and leadership provided by the principal (Hall, Rutherford, Hord, and Huling 1984; Hord and Hall 1987). When the principal was active in planning and guiding the change process, the principal selected a person on the school roster to fill the second CF role; when the principal did not direct much energy and activity toward change, a central office person appeared to supply action.

The principals most effective in implementing change were team-oriented, working collegially with their second CFs. Interestingly, each of these team members provided an equal number of interventions. The principals who were somewhat more management oriented than leadership oriented did more of the support work themselves, leaving their second CFs with less involvement. The principals who offered little active support for change did few interventions for teachers. While the district-based second CF usually did much more to compensate for the principal's lack of involvement, this approach was the least effective in supporting change efforts. For obvious reasons, the assistance provided by building-based (rather than district-based) CFs is likely to be more efficient, effective, and well received by teachers.

Frequently, we also found third CFs. Typically, these were teachers whose roles were less formalized, but whose help was substantial and sought by their peers. These third CFs modeled the use of the new program, disseminated information to other teachers, interpreted messages, and provided clarification about what activities to perform or how.

First, second, and third CFs organize themselves and build structures to work together as a change facilitator team. In some schools, they may meet each week to review data about the school improvement process, generate ideas, and plan who will do what during the ensuing week. When they meet again, they debrief to ascertain what went well and what needs more attention. In other schools we observed a more hierarchical organization of facilitators: the first CF (the principal) appeared to interact only with the second CF, who in turn related to the third CF. All communications flowed through this "chain of command." Whether the team of CFs has a "flat," or horizontal, collegial structure or a more hierarchical one, however, the important aspects to remember are what they need to do as a group.

We identified a fourth category of change facilitator: the external facilitator. External facilitators bring particular innovation-related expertise not found among the school-based members of the CF team; the district office external facilitator links the school to district office resources and serves as a communication line between the school and district office. In addition, the external CF serves as an advocate for the school outside the school setting.

Figure 5.4 arranges the functions of interventions carried out by change facilitator teams into a single planning chart. It is important to make sure that the facilitator team, collectively, addresses all of the intervention functions listed on the chart. This does not necessarily mean, however, that one particular team member must always be responsible for supplying one particular kind of intervention. Rather, the tasks may vary, depending upon who is most capable or available. Function assignments should not be rigid; accomplishing the interventions is the primary goal.

Some functions can be carried out most effectively by the principal. By virtue of the principal's pivotal position, what the principal does often carries more weight and influence than what others do. Principals, however, do not have the time to do all the work of facilitating change by themselves. Therefore, certain functions should receive the principal's attention as priorities. These are: sanctioning the change, identifying it as a priority, providing resources, and endorsing the position and activities of other CF team members. If the principal is active in no other way, she or he should take responsibility for these functions. They cannot be accomplished as powerfully by anyone else.

Figure 5.4. The Importance of Who Does What for Successful Change

Change Facilitating Team Members

FUNCTIONS	First CF (principal)	Second CF	Third CF	External CFs
1. Sanctioning/ continued back up	xxxx	xx		xx
2. Providing resources	xxx	xx		x
3. Technical coaching	x	xx	x	x
4. Monitoring/ follow up	xx	xx	x	
5. Training	x	x		xx
6. Reinforcing	xx	xxx	x	x
7. Pushing	xx	xx	x	x
8. Telling others	xx	x		x
9. Approving adaptations	xx	x		x

Legend: x, xx, xxx, xxxx = Degree of importance

From: Hall and Hord 1987

Through our studies, we were able to identify characteristics of effective CF team operation (Hall and Hord 1986). First, the members of the team are in continuous, typically informal, contact with each other and with the school staff. Second, each member of the CF team complements the role of the others; collectively, through sharing and overlapping of assignments, they take responsibility for all the functions. Third, each member shares a common view of the goals of the school improvement project; there is clarity and agreement about the objectives and directions for the change process.

Open planning is a fourth characteristic of the team, with all members sharing and discussing what can be done. Planning is ongoing, constantly reviewed and revised through informal conversations and regularly scheduled team meetings. Fifth, planning, decisions, and actions are taken with the total improvement game plan in mind; this facilitates consistent actions by the various CFs. Collegiality, a sixth aspect, is an inherent element in each of the foregoing five characteristics.

Because sufficient knowledge, communication, and a shared agenda exist, it is possible for each member of the team to gain from the work of fellow members, resulting in a total process of change that is greater than the simple addition of the efforts of each individual facilitator—this "geometric summing" is a seventh factor of CF teams. The eighth factor is team complementarity: increased use of members' strengths but decreased emphasis on individuals, and a willing filling of gaps and anticipation of what other team members will be doing. All of these factors contribute to the ninth: positive professionalism and enthusiasm for the innovation, for the capabilities of the school, and the activities that are taking place. Of course we believe also that all CFs need to be familiar with SoC, LoU, and IC, the CBAM tools that can help guide and clarify the change process.

Initiating the Change Process

In this chapter we have tried to convey the significant and vital role that you play as change facilitator. Your tasks are not easy. Though they may appear deceptively simple in our tidy charts and chapters, they are complex undertakings. If you are seeking to use our tools and techniques for the first time, we suggest starting with a small team of colleagues who will serve as CFs. A starting point might be to read and discuss this book. Then in consultation with teachers, decide on a modest school change to implement, an effort that can be successful for everyone. Then go from there.

One last thing we might suggest to you: learn "mushroom detection." What, you may ask, is that? Just like mushrooms that pop up unexpectedly after a spring shower, efforts to facilitate change may, from time to time, produce some surprising—and unplanned—results. Be sensitive to these possibilities, take corrective actions as you can, and learn to thrive in a changing landscape.

Questions Commonly Asked about
Facilitators and Interventions

Q: *Does it matter who my second CF is?*

A: Yes, it should be someone who is enthusiastic about the change to be facilitated and who has the respect and regard of the school staff. Obviously, it should be someone who is regularly available and accessible to work with teachers. Someone with whom you can work collegially and comfortably, as well as someone who has knowledge of and expertise with the change, is certainly desirable.

Q: *Are principals expected to do training?*

A: When principals do training, it can be very effective for they know their teachers and their situation. Even if principals are not doing training themselves, they can be involved: they can make arrangements with others, such as central office "experts" or staff developers, to do the training. Studies have shown that if principals attend training sessions with their teachers and engage in the training activities with them, change occurs more effectively.

Q: *Is it possible for the same person who evaluates teachers' performance also to monitor their implementation of change?*

A: Yes, it is possible to do this effectively if several conditions are met. First, the principal or other facilitator who is monitoring should make it clear that the monitoring activities are for the purpose of school improvement and not for teacher assessment. Second, the monitoring purpose should be made clear to the teacher: that it will form the basis for providing support and assistance to the teacher. Third, the help and support should be immediately available and visible following the monitoring activity so that the facilitator is seen as just that—a helper, not an evaluator.

Q: *If a game plan is made according to the GPCs and long- and short-range objectives, is that all there is to it?*

A: Well, no. We suggest that obstacles or barriers, and any problems that can be anticipated related to the particular change, be considered, and that the planning take those things into account. Particular policies may need developing, for example. And, of course, the plan should consider the people who will do the changing—and their developing SoC, LoU, and IC patterns during the change process.

Q: *Once you have an intervention game plan, is it necessary to abide by it 100 percent?*

A: No, most football coaches begin with a plan for conducting the game, but if the plan is moving the team closer to defeat than to victory, a coach will shift to a contingency plan. The game plan components provide a framework for making a long-range plan that is not sacred. In other words, a game plan is the best starting point that can be devised on currently available information and thinking. If some parts do not work well, they should be adjusted and changed as the situation dictates.

6.
Last Words: Implications & Our Central Message

THIS BOOK HAS BEEN ABOUT TAKING CHARGE OF CHANGE, OF LEADING and facilitating the process and the people involved in it. Its most important message has been to direct attention to the needs of the people who must change.

In case we have not been clear, we take this last opportunity to distinguish between the applications of the CBAM as a tool for change facilitation—which is the focus of this book—and the model's application for research and evaluation. Much more thorough understanding and training are required for the latter than for clinical applications. We have not attempted here to lay out all the bits and pieces of our model. Where detail and technical processes are lacking, we have cited references for additional reading. Our goal has been to provide enough basic concepts, tools, and procedures to launch you as a facilitator. A more technical treatment of the CBAM (Hall and Hord 1987) is available for those who wish to delve further, especially those who are eager for a more scholarly discussion of the concepts and for a more extensive report of research results.

Our enthusiasm throughout this text may have implied that, once equipped with CBAM's tools, the facilitator has enormous control over

response

the change process and can save the day through data gathering and planning. Perhaps control is not as much to the point as understanding. Understanding helps the CF keep the fingers firmly on the pulse of the process and permits more effective responses as the process unfolds.

In this context, it is important that we emphasize that personal concerns are okay. The key to successful facilitation is to personalize one's interventions by focusing attention on the concerns of those engaged in the change process and accepting those concerns as legitimate reflections of changes in progress. This contrasts sharply with the more instinctive tendency of managers to direct change from the perspective of their own concerns and objectives. Policymakers as well are known to reach decisions and to direct actions based on policy-level concerns, and they should at the very least adjust their expectations for results to take into account the concerns of those affected by the change.

Policymakers and administrators contemplating change should consider also the questions of who will facilitate the facilitators. Principals, central office staff, even teachers find themselves in new roles as members of facilitation teams, and they too experience the change process as they learn these new skills. Once again, the understanding offered by the CBAM concepts provides a tool for gauging progress and providing encouragement and stimulation.

Understanding of change should also lead policymakers to a better appreciation of the complexities of the very human process of change and of the demands that process imposes at every level of the system. Innovations are often thought of as single things—an effective school program, for example—when they may in fact be bundles that include five, seven, eight, nine, or more components. There are limits to the number of bundles and bundle components that people or institutions can handle effectively at one time.

We hope your reading of these chapters has given you some "Aha!s." It has been our intention to provide new insights and understandings of school change and new meaning about the roles people and their personal needs play in the process. If we have struck a familiar chord—a note that rings true with your own experience—then you will have added new validity to the CBAM and we will have succeeded in our task.

References and Relevant Readings

Information about these references may be obtained from:

Southwest Educational Development Laboratory
211 East Seventh Street
Austin, TX 78701
(512) 476-6861

Draughon, B.S., and S.M. Hord. "Even Champions Have Coaches: Principals Provide Professional Development for Their Peers." *Journal of Staff Development* 7, 2 (1986): 81–90.

Gall, M.D., G. Fielding, D. Schalock, W.W. Charters, Jr., and J.M. Wilcynski. *Involving the Principal in Teachers' Staff Development: Effects on the Quality of Mathematics Instruction in Elementary Schools.* Eugene: Center for Educational Policy and Management, University of Oregon, 1984.

Gersten, R., and D. Carnine. *Administrative and Supervisory Support Functions for the Implementation of Effective Educational Programs for Low Income Students.* Eugene: Center for Educational Policy and Management, University of Oregon, 1981.

Hall, G.E. "The Concerns-based Approach for Facilitating Change." *Educational Horizons* 57 (1979): 202–208.

Hall, G.E., A.A. George, and W.L. Rutherford. *Measuring Stages of Concern about the Innovation: A Manual for the Use of the SoC Questionnaire.* Austin: Research and Development Center for Teacher Education, University of Texas at Austin, 1979.

Hall, G.E., and S.M. Hord. "Analyzing What Change Facilitators Do: The Intervention Taxonomy." *Knowledge: Creation, Diffusion, Utilization* 5, 3 (1984): 275–307.

Hall, G.E., and S.M. Hord. "Configurations of School-based Leadership Teams." Paper presented at the annual meeting of the American Educational Research Association, San Francisco, 1986.

Hall, G.E., and S.M. Hord. *Change in Schools: Facilitating the Process.* Albany: State University of New York Press, 1987.

Hall, G.E., S. Hord, W.L. Rutherford, S.F. Loucks, L.L. Huling, and S.A. Heck. *Workshop on Innovation Configurations: The Trainer's Manual.* Austin: Research and Development Center for Teacher Education, University of Texas at Austin, 1982.

Hall, G.E., and S.F. Loucks. "Program Definition and Adaptation: Implications for Inservice." *Journal of Research and Development in Education* 14, 2 (1981): 46–58.

Hall, G.E., S.F. Loucks, W.L. Rutherford, and B. Newlove. "Levels of Use of the Innovation: A Framework for Analyzing Innovation Adoption." *Journal of Teacher Education* 24 (1975): 52–56.

Hall, G.E., W.L. Rutherford, S.M. Hord, and L.L. Huling. "Effects of Three Principal Styles on School Improvement." *Educational Leadership* 41, 5 (1984): 22–29.

Heck, S., S.M. Stiegelbauer, G.E. Hall, and S.F. Loucks. *Measuring Innovation Configurations: Procedures and Applications.* Austin: Research and Development Center for Teacher Education, University of Texas at Austin, 1981.

Hord, S.M. *Evaluating Educational Innovation.* London: Croom Helm, 1987.

Hord, S.M., and G.E. Hall. "Three Images: What Principals Do in Curriculum Implementation." *Curriculum Inquiry* 17, 1 (1987): 55–98.

Hord, S.M., and L. Huling-Austin. "Effective Curriculum Implementation: Some Promising New Insights." *Elementary School Journal* 87, 1 (1986): 97–115.

Hord, S.M., and S.F. Loucks. *A Concerns-based Model for the Delivery of Inservice.* Austin: Research and Development Center for Teacher Education, University of Texas at Austin, 1980.

Hord, S.M., S.M. Stiegelbauer, and G.E. Hall. "How Principals Work with Other Change Facilitators." *Education and Urban Society* 17, 1 (1984) 89–109.

Loucks, S.F. *Levels of Use of the ISCS Curriculum as Demonstrated by Junior*

High School Teachers: A Case Study Approach. Austin: Research and Development Center for Teacher Education, University of Texas at Austin, 1977.

Loucks, S.F., B.H. Newlove, and G.E. Hall. *Measuring Levels of Use of the Innovation: A Manual for Trainers, Interviewers, and Raters.* Austin: Research and Development Center for Teacher Education, University of Texas at Austin, 1975.

Newlove, B.W., and G.E. Hall. *A Manual for Assessing Open-ended Statements of Concern about an Innovation.* Austin: Research and Development Center for Teacher Education, University of Texas at Austin, 1976.

Rutherford, W.L. "School Principals as Effective Leaders." *Phi Delta Kappan* 67, 1 (1985) 31–34.

Relevant Readings

Information about these readings may be obtained from:
Southwest Educational Development Laboratory
211 East Seventh Street
Austin, TX 78701
(512) 476-6861

Collaboration for Change
Hall, G.E., and H. Pratt. *There Really Can be a Symbiotic Relationship Between Researchers and Practitioners: The Marriage of a National R&D Center and a Large School District.* Austin: Research and Development Center for Teacher Education, University of Texas at Austin, 1983. (ERIC ED 250 816.)

Hord, S.M. "A Synthesis of Research on Organizational Collaboration." *Educational Leadership* 43, 5 (1986): 22–26.

Hord, S.M., and W.L. Rutherford. "An Educational Change Model: Implementing Teacher Corps Interventions." In *School Improvement and In-service Education: Issues and Practices,* edited by R. Olivero. Washington, D.C.: National Teacher Corps, 1980.

Facilitators and Facilitation
Hall, G.E., and S.M. Hord. *Configurations of School-based Leadership Teams.* Austin: Research and Development Center for Teacher Education, University of Texas at Austin, 1986.

Hall, G.E., and S.M. Hord. *Change in Schools: Facilitating the Process.* Ithaca: State University of New York Press, 1987.

Hall, G.E., S.M. Hord, and S. Putman. *The Role of District Office Personnel in High School Change*. Austin: Research and Development Center for Teacher Education, University of Texas at Austin, 1985.

Hord, S.M. *Evaluating Educational Innovations*. London: Croom Helm, 1987.

Hord, S.M., and E.M. Diaz-Ortiz. "Beyond the Principal: Can the Department Head Supply Leadership for Change in High Schools?" In *Research on Internal Change Facilitation*, edited by R. Vandenberge and G. Hall. Leuven, Belgium: Acco, 1987.

Hord, S.M., and S.F. Loucks. *A Concerns-based Model for the Delivery of Inservice*. Austin: Research and Development Center for Teacher Education, University of Texas at Austin, 1980.

Hord, S.M., and S.C. Murphy. *The High School Department Head: Powerful or Powerless in Guiding Change?* Austin: Research and Development Center for Teacher Education, University of Texas at Austin, 1985.

Rutherford, W.L., S.M. Hord, L.L. Huling, and G.E. Hall. *Change Facilitators: In Search of Understanding Their Role*. Austin: Research and Development Center for Teacher Education, University of Texas at Austin, 1983.

High School Change

Hall, G.E., and S.M. Hord. "High School Change: Boarding House or Hotel Restaurant Approach?" *The Northeast Perspective* 1, 6 (1984): 1–2, 7.

Hall, G.E., and S.M. Hord. "Change in the High School: Many Cooks in the Kitchen." *Resources and Practice* 3, 2 (December 1984—January 1985): 1–3.

Hall, G.E., S.M. Hord, W.L. Rutherford, and L.L. Huling. "Change in High Schools: Rolling Stones or Asleep at the Wheel?" *Educational Leadership* 41, 6 (1984): 58–62.

Hord, S.M., and W.L. Rutherford. "Dogs Can't Sing? Good News, a Dash of Optimism and High School Change." *The High School Journal* 69, 1 (1985): 16–20.

Rutherford, W. L., and L. Huling-Austin. "The National Commission Reports: A Comparison of Proposed and Actual Changes in High Schools." *Journal of Staff Development* 5, 2 (December 1984): 40–50.

Innovation Configurations

Hall, G.E., and S.F. Loucks. "Program Definition and Adaptation: Implications for Inservice." *Journal of Research and Development in Education* 14, 2 (1981): 46–58.

Heck, S., S.M. Stiegelbauer, G.E. Hall, and S.F. Loucks. *Measuring Innovation Configurations: Procedures and Applications*. Austin: Research and Development Center for Teacher Education, University of Texas at Austin, 1981.

Hord, S.M. *A Manual for Using Innovation Configurations to Assess Teacher Development Programs.* Austin: Research and Development Center for Teacher Education, University of Texas at Austin, 1986.

Interventions

Hall, G.E. "The Concerns-based Approach to Facilitating Change." *Educational Horizons* 57, 4 (1979): 202–208.

Hall, G.E., and S.M. Hord. "A Framework for Analyzing What Change Facilitators Do: The Intervention Taxonomy." *Knowledge: Creation, Diffusion, Utilization* 5, 3 (1984): 275–307.

Hord, S.M. *Analyzing Administrators' Intervention Behaviors.* Austin: Research and Development Center for Teacher Education, University of Texas at Austin, 1981. (ERIC ED 231 060.)

Hord, S.M., and L. Huling-Austin. "Effective Curriculum Implementation: Some Promising New Insights." *The Elementary School Journal* 87, 1 (1986): 97–115.

Levels of Use

Hall, G.E., S.F. Loucks, W.L. Rutherford, and B. Newlove. "Levels of Use of the Innovation: A Framework for Analyzing Innovation Adoption." *Journal of Teacher Education* 29, 1 (1975): 52–56.

Loucks, S.F. *Levels of Use of the ISCS Curriculum as Demonstrated by Junior High School Teachers: A Case Study Approach.* Austin: Research and Development Center for Teacher Education, University of Texas at Austin, 1977.

Loucks, S.F., B.W. Newlove, and G.E. Hall. *Measuring Levels of Use of the Innovation: A Manual for Trainers, Interviewers, and Raters.* Austin: Research and Development Center for Teacher Education, University of Texas at Austin, 1975.

Principals and Change

Hall, G.E., and S.M. Hord. "Change Facilitator Style." In *Instructional Leadership Handbook*, edited by J.W. Keefe and J.M. Jenkins. Reston, Va.: National Association of Secondary School Principals, 1984.

Hall, G.E., W.L. Rutherford, S.M. Hord, and L.L. Huling. "Effects of Three Principal Styles on School Improvement." *Educational Leadership*, 41, 5 (1984): 22–29.

Hord, S.M. "The Changing Role of Principals: Impressions of an Innocent Abroad." *The Review* (London). In press.

Hord, S.M., and G.E. Hall. "Three Images: What Principals Do in Curriculum Implementation." *Curriculum Inquiry* 17,1 (1987): 55–89.

Huling, L.L., G.E. Hall, and S.M. Hord. "Effects of Principal Interventions on Teachers During the Change Process." Austin: Research and Development Center for Teacher Education, University of Texas at Austin, 1982.

Huling, L., G.E. Hall, S.M. Hord, and W.L. Rutherford. "A Multi-Dimensional Approach to Assessing Implemention Success." Austin: Research and Development Center for Teacher Education, University of Texas at Austin, 1983.

Murphy, S.C., and S.M. Hord. "A Pathway to Instructional Improvement: Priming the Territory." In *The Rural and Small School Principalship: Practice, Research and Vision*, edited by E. Ducharme and D. Fleming. Chelmsford, Mass.: Northeast Regional Exchange, 1985.

Rutherford, W.L. "Styles and Behaviors of Elementary School Principals and Their Relationship to School Improvement." *Education and Urban Society* 17,1 (1984): 9–28.

Rutherford, W.L. "School Principals as Effective Leaders." *Phi Delta Kappan* 69,1 (1985): 31–34.

Rutherford, W.L., S.C. Murphy, and S.M. Hord. "School Management, School Development, School Improvement in the United States with New Light from an Old Lamp: Castleton High School." In *The School Leader and School Improvement: Case Studies from Ten OECD Countries*, edited by C. Hopes. Leuven, Belgium: Acco, 1986.

Stego, E., K. Gielen, R. Glatter, and S. Hord, eds. *The Role of School Leaders in School Improvement*. Leuven, Belgium: Acco, 1987.

Second CF

Hord, S.M., G.E. Hall, and S.M. Stiegelbauer. *Principals Don't Do It Alone: The Role of the Consigliere*. Austin: Research and Development Center for Teacher Education, University of Texas at Austin, 1983.

Hord, S.M., S.M. Stiegelbauer, and G.E. Hall. "How Principals Work with Other Change Facilitators." *Education and Urban Society* 17,1 (1984): 89–109.

Hord, S.M., S.M. Stiegelbauer, and G.E. Hall. "Principals Don't Do It Alone: Researchers Discover Second Change Facilitators Active in School Improvement Efforts." *R&DCTE Review* 2,3 (1984): 1–2, 5.

Stages of Concern

Hall, G.E. "The Concerns-based Approach to Facilitating Change." *Educational Horizons* 57,4 (1979): 202–208.

Hall, G.E., A.A. George, and W.L. Rutherford. *Measuring Stages of Concern about the Innovation: A Manual for the Use of the SoC Questionnaire*. Austin: Research and Development Center for Teacher Education, University of Texas at Austin, 1979.

Newlove, B.W., and G.E. Hall. *A Manual for Assessing Open-ended State-ments of Concern about an Innovation.* Austin: Research and Development Center for Teacher Education, University of Texas at Austin, 1976.

Training for Principals and Facilitators
Blum, R.E., and J.A. Butler, eds. *School Leader Development for School Improvement.* Leuven, Belgium: Acco, 1987.
Blum, R.E., and S.M. Hord. "Using Research as a Basis for School Improvement in Alaska." *Journal of Staff Development* 4,1 (1983): 136–151.
Draughon, B., and S.M. Hord. "Even Champions Have Coaches: Princi-pals Provide Professional Development to Their Peers." *The Journal of Staff Development* 7,2 (1986): 81–90.
Hord, S.M., and L.L. Huling-Austin. *Preparing Administrators to be Effec-tive Facilitators of School Improvement Inservice.* New York: National Council of States on Inservice Education, Syracuse University, 1985.
Hord, S.M., and L.L. Huling-Austin. "Implementation Skills for School Leaders: A Training Program for Facilitating Change." In *School Leader Development for School Improvement,* edited by R.E. Blum and J.A. Butler. Leuven, Belgium: Acco. Forthcoming.
Hord, S.M., and J.C. Thurber. "Helping Principals Use Tools to Support Their Leadership Roles in School Improvement." In *Preparing School Leaders for Educational Improvement: An International Perspective,* edited by K. Leithwood, W. Rutherford, and R. van der Vegt. London: Croom Helm, 1987.
Hord, S.M., J.C. Thurber, and G.E. Hall. "Helping Administrators Change: Tools for Leadership." *The Developer,* May, 1981, 2–11.
Rutherford, W.L., S.M. Hord, and J.C. Thurber. "Preparing Principals for Leadership Roles in School Improvement." *Education and Urban Society,* 17,1 (1984): 29–48.

About the Authors

Gene E. Hall is a Professor in the Department of Educational Leadership and Director of the Research and Development Center for School Improvement, College of Education, University of Florida at Gainesville. His present research and teaching activities are centered on the school principalship and the role of district office personnel as facilitators for school improvement. From 1968 to 1986, he was a staff member in the Research and Development Center for Teacher Education at the University of Texas at Austin. During this time he was the principal architect of research and development activities for the Concerns Based Adoption Model. During his last two years at R&DCTE he also served as Center Director.

Shirley M. Hord is Senior Development Associate at the Southwest Educational Development Laboratory in Austin, Texas, where she designs and coordinates professional development activities related to educational change, school improvement, and school leadership; in addition, she is field coordinator for a multi-year rural school improvement project in the Lab's region. In her prior role as a Co-Director of Research on the Improvement Process at the Research and Development Center for Teacher Education at the University of Texas at Austin, she administered and conducted research on school improvement and the role of school leadership in school change. She serves on the editorial and publications board of *The Journal of Teacher Education* and as the U.S. representative to the OECD/CERI International School Improvement Project, an international effort to develop research, training, and policy initiatives that will support local school improvement practices.

William L. Rutherford is an Associate Professor in the Department of Curriculum and Instruction at the University of Texas at Austin. In the College of Education, he teaches graduate courses in staff development, instructional leadership, and implementing change, and supervises undergraduate student teachers. For more than 15 years he served on the research team at the Research and Development Center for Teacher Education that developed the Concerns-Based Adoption Model.

Leslie Huling-Austin is an Associate Professor at Southwest Texas State University in San Marcos, where she teaches in the Secondary Education Program and is a researcher for the LBJ Institute for the Improvement of Teaching and Learning. From 1981 to 1986 she was a senior staff member at the Research and Development Center for Teacher Education at the University of Texas at Austin where she conducted research on school change and provided training for school leaders in facilitating the school improvement process. In addition, she conducted research on beginning teachers and teacher induction programs in her role as principal investigator of the Model Teacher Induction Project study. In this capacity she coordinated a national Teacher Induction Network and managed a national collaborative effort involving 26 institutions across the U.S.